Ripple and Stablecoins: Building Banks of Tomorrow

Use Cases on International Remittance, Capital and Money Markets, Swaps, Micropayments, Trade Finance, Islamic Finance, and Stablecoins

by
Debajani Mohanty

FIRST EDITION 2019

Copyright © BPB Publications, India

ISBN: 978-93-89423-198

LIMITS OF LIABILITY AND DISCLAIMER OF WARRANTY

Distributors:

BPB PUBLICATIONS
20, Ansari Road, Darya Ganj
New Delhi-110002
Ph: 23254990/23254991

DECCAN AGENCIES
4-3-329, Bank Street,
Hyderabad-500195
Ph: 24756967/24756400

MICRO MEDIA
Shop No. 5, Mahendra Chambers,
150 DN Rd. Next to Capital Cinema,
V.T. (C.S.T.) Station, MUMBAI-400 001
Ph: 22078296/22078297

BPB BOOK CENTRE
376 Old Lajpat Rai Market,
Delhi-110006
Ph: 23861747

Published by Manish Jain for BPB Publications, 20 Ansari Road, Darya Ganj, New Delhi-110002 and Printed by him at Repro India Ltd, Mumbai

About the Author

 **Debajani Mohanty** is a Solution Architect who has been involved in large-scale projects and has built many scalable enterprises for B2B and B2C products, right from conceptualization to marketing, in varied domains such as travel, e-governance, e-commerce, and BFSI. Writing complex technical articles in an easy-to-understand language and with high readability is her forte that has earned her close to fifteen thousand followers on social media.

Debajani has authored the bestseller *Blockchain from Concept to Execution* by BPB publications, one of the few books in the IT industry that has been translated to other international languages such as German and Chinese. She has also written *Ethereum for Architects* and *Developers* and *R3 Corda for Architects and Developers*, published by Apress and Springer Nature, which have been well received by the industry.

Debajani is a global Blockchain pioneer and leader who has architected many unique products that are in the pilot and production phase in India as well as the international market. Also, she has been awarded and appreciated by business leaders globally. She has been a keynote speaker at PACT Forum (Philadelphia, USA), NASSCOM, UNICOM, Amity, and many other prestigious events.

Debajani is a women's rights activist and was felicitated by Nobel Peace prize winner Mr. Kailash Satyarthi with the prestigious Aarya Award for her outstanding contributions to women empowerment in the field of literature.

Follow her on Twitter: https://twitter.com/debimr75

Follow her on LinkedIn: https://www.linkedin.com/in/debajanimohantypmp/

Reviewer

 **Hugh Macmillen** has over twenty-five years of trading experience in the interest rate markets in Europe. Over the past three years he has been experimenting with alternative interbank payment systems such as XRP with the aim to reduce costs and enable intraday transactions in the unsecured money market.

Hugh Macmillen is the founder of Instimatch AG Baar in Switzerland, a ground-breaking, peer-to-peer liquidity network for institutional borrowers and lenders. Instimatch Global AG was nominated among the top 5 start-ups in 2019 by the prestigious FN London News Network in the UK, under the category of Fixed Income.

Instimatch was one of the first MVP DAPPs to be registered on the Ethereum project in 2015.

Currently, Instimatch is experimenting with R3 Corda and XRP Settler for intraday payments and cross-border interbank payments. Through the adoption of this technology, significant savings can be made for their clientele as expensive nostro accounts would no longer be required.

Acknowledgements

This book through and through is an ode to my mother Mrs. Nirupama Mohanty, who, despite an ongoing treatment of breast cancer, has stood by my side in my struggle to cope up with family, finish projects on time, and, at the same time, gather content for my manuscript. With her support through thick and thin of life, each of my books gets better and better, surpassing my own expectations and benefitting thousands of my readers who eagerly look forward to my upcoming work.

Preface

More than a decade ago, after staying in England for almost five years, I returned to my homeland, India. I had to take the help of the international remittance system of banks for transferring the fortune that I had earned staying abroad. The waiting period was long and painful, and after almost a week's time, I had a sigh of relief as the local bank in India informed me that the transaction was through. However, the relief didn't last long; what I ended up receiving in my Indian account made me shed buckets of tears. The fees and cost of remittance over the wire had cost me almost 8% of the entire amount, which was huge! That was when I made up my mind to work in this area, to help improve the flawed and dated system, so that my small contribution would help improve the global remittance and related trading systems some day in future. I am glad that the day has finally come.

As per a Finextra news report back in 2016, people across the world send more than $155 trillion across borders, and this number is on an exponential rise year after year.

"With over $155 trillion of cross-border payments being made between businesses annually, it is crucial that we continue to innovate to make international payments easier and faster, not just for our clients but also for the future of the payments industry," says Gautam Jain, global head, digitisation and client access, transaction banking, Standard Chartered. "As a leading international bank committed to facilitating trade, commerce and investments, this partnership will go a long way in progressing our digitisation agenda to develop innovative solutions for our clients."

https://www.finextra.com/newsarticle/29445/ripple-scores-55-million-funding-round-adds-new-bank-members

Also, according to a recent article published by the World Bank on April 8, 2019, India is the topmost receiver of remittances from across the world.

Among countries, the top remittance recipients were India with $79 billion, followed by China ($67 billion), Mexico ($36 billion), the Philippines ($34 billion), and Egypt ($29 billion).

https://www.worldbank.org/en/news/press-release/2019/04/08/record-high-remittances-sent-globally-in-2018

Hence, being an Indian and a solution architect, as well as a writer, I felt it was my responsibility to bring awareness in this space so that next-generation payment technologies would be perceived and accepted in the market for mass adoption.

Post the remarkable success of my three books on Blockchain, I have been invited to many panel discussions to offer my view on how Blockchain as a technology can bring a new future to the existing business processes. I often advise that, it does not matter how smooth the business processes are, if the payment leg is not efficient, it would bring unnecessary delay in achieving the end results.

Interestingly though, many CXOs and business heads still do not have a full understanding of the limitations of the existing payment systems that jeopardize business processes in the industry and, at the same time, are unsure of the advantages cutting-edge technologies can offer by revising their age-old remittance systems. This book would be a good starter for them, not only to learn Ripple, but to envision the future of the payment industry and how that would help the entire business ecosystem to progress towards *Bank 4.0*. Be it trade finance, e-Auction, micro-funding, money market, or Islamic finance, the use cases reviewed in this book will educate readers about how this emerging technology could benefit in rebuilding their business boundaries.

This book is written for all IT professionals. It starts with the loopholes in the existing banking and payment industry that have led to the invention of Bitcoin and Blockchain, followed by Ripple. The book focuses on Ripple's architecture and development APIs with adequate examples. In later chapters, the book reviews different use cases that will greatly help business leaders, analysts, and developers alike.

This book has also given me the opportunity to learn the entire ecosystem of Ripple, thus helping me in advocating the benefits of Ripple adoption to my clients, and eventually helping us all gradually to move towards achieving a common dream —*Bank 4.0 and beyond.*

Errata

We take immense pride in our work at BPB Publications and follow best practices to ensure the accuracy of our content to provide with an indulging reading experience to our subscribers. Our readers are our mirrors, and we use their inputs to reflect and improve upon human errors if any, occurred during the publishing processes involved. To let us maintain the quality and help us reach out to any readers who might be having difficulties due to any unforeseen errors, please write to us at :

errata@bpbonline.com

Your support, suggestions and feedbacks are highly appreciated by the BPB Publications' Family.

Table of Contents

1. Evolution of Payment Systems.. 1

    Babylon to Bitcoin: History of Payments 1

    Evolution of banks.. 3

    Pain points of modern banking system....................................... 4

    Credibility of banks before and after 2007 crisis...................... 4

    Pre-Blockchain instant money transfer solutions 5

    Bitcoin: The end of money... 6

    What criteria did Bitcoin lack for cross-border remittance?.... 6

    Blockchain technology 7

    Advantages of Blockchain 8

    What is Ripple?... 10

    XRP 12

    Advantages of Ripple 14

    Disadvantages of Ripple... 15

    Why are banks still hesitant to adopt Ripple?......................... 15

    Misconceptions and unknown facts of Ripple 15

    FinTechs on XRP ecosystem 19

    Summary... 19

    Questions 20

    Answers 21

    References 22

    Some other great resources for reference are as follows: 22

2. Ripple Architecture 23

    How does international remittance work? 23

    Intrabank money transfer.. 24

    Interbank money transfer.. 24

    International money transfer 25

    SWIFT.. 26

    SWIFT pain points.. 28

Introduction of SWIFT global payment
innovation (gpi) 29

Liquidity issue with nostro accounts 30

Ripple: The new-age payment system 31

XRP Ledger 31

Consensus in XRP Ledger 31

Rippled Server 33

XRP 33

Drops 34

Issued currencies 34

Trust lines 34

Freezing issued currencies 35

RippleNet 35

xVia (standard access) 36

xCurrent (full access) 37

xRapid 39

xCurrent 4.0 41

Where else can Ripple be used? 42

SWIFT versus Ripple 43

Ripple and R3 Corda: The golden alliance 44

Distributed ledger 45

R3 Corda features 46

Summary 49

Questions 49

Answers 51

References 51

3. Development with RippleNet and XRP 53

Important factors of XRP account 54

Running a local rippled validating server 55

XRP Ledger endpoints 56

Retrieve account information (account_info) 56

Transfer XRPs between accounts (payment and submit) 60

Partial payment.. 69

Illegal Use Case... 70

Legal Use Case 71

Cross-currency payments... 71

Escrow payment 72

Checks 79

Payment channels... 81

Create XRP account in production.. 83

Software wallet 83

Mobile wallet... 83

Hardware wallet 83

How does one send XRPs?... 84

How does one buy XRPs? 84

Summary... 85

Questions 86

4. Use Case: Micropayments 89

Business scenario: Amazon and PayPal... 89

Challenges in micropayments 90

Examples... 90

IoT messaging 90

Charity.. 91

Services... 91

Microfinance.. 91

Solution with Ripple/XRP 91

XRP for micropayments in news... 92

Summary... 92

References 92

5. Use Case: Instant Security Settlement in Stock Market..................... 93

Instant settlement: The golden goose 95

Solution 95

Tokenization model 96

Ripple-based settlement 96

Forex rates 97

Advantages 98

Summary 99

References 99

6. Use Case: Settlement for Intraday Trading in Money Market 101

Capital market 102

Money market 102

Why is a strong money market important for intraday trading? 103

Challenges in money market 103

Business scenario 104

Complete Blockchain solution 104

Advantages 107

Summary 107

References 107

7. Use Case: Derivatives and Swaps 109

Types of derivatives 109

Forward 110

Warrants 111

Swaps 111

Challenges in derivatives 111

Solution 112

Advantages 113

Summary 114

8. Use Case: Trade Finance 115

What is trade finance? 115

Use Case: Petroleum trade 115

Mitigating manufacturing and payment risks 117

Getting business insured 117

Business process flow 118

Challenges in international trading 120

Parties 121

Currency 121

Payment 121

Solution 121

Advantages.. 122

Complete Blockchain solution... 123

Live Use Case 124

Euro Exim Bank 124

Standard Chartered Bank 124

Summary.. 124

References 125

Some other great resources for reference are as follows: 125

9. Stablecoins 127

What are Stablecoins? 127

Types of Stablecoins 128

Backed by valuable collaterals.. 129

Backed by fiat currency 129

Backed by crypto currency.. 130

Backed by no collateral 130

Most popular Stablecoins of the world 131

Tether... 131

JPM Coin: A Stablecoin by JPMorgan.. 131

Libra: A Stablecoin by Facebook... 132

Stablecoin by Swiss Stock Exchange... 134

Stablecoin by Binance 134

Ripple versus Stablecoins— who will win?..................................... 135

Pros of Ripple.. 135

Cons of Ripple... 135

Pros of Stablecoins.. 135

Cons of Stablecoins... 135

Summary.. 136

Questions 136

Answers 137

References 138

Some other great resources for reference are as follows: 138

10. **Use Case: Islamic Banking** 139

What is Islamic banking? 139

Crypto currencies in Islamic finance 140

Islamic version of crypto currency 140

Scenario: Gold tokenization 140

Data 142

System architecture diagram 142

Transactions on Ledger 145

Advantages 146

Summary 147

References 147

11. **Banks of Tomorrow** 149

Biggest banks of the world 149

Live use cases: Continents and countries 152

North America 152

South America 153

Europe 153

Oceania 154

Asia 154

Crypto ban in India! 157

Conclusion 159

Summary 161

References 161

Some other great resources for reference are as follows: 165

CHAPTER 1

Evolution of Payment Systems

International trading is complex, so is international funds transfer. One of the biggest inventions in recent times is *Internet of Value*, a sincere attempt by a young FinTech called Ripple with a monumental objective to bring equilibrium in the financial and economic space.

In this chapter, we will discuss the different payment systems used in human history and their inherent flaws that have led to technological innovations of the century, such as Bitcoin, Altcoins, Ripple, as well as different Stablecoins. While there is so much of debate going on everywhere on the adoption of Ripple technology, it would be a nice starting point to know some of the misconceptions around it, and the torchbearers of this cutting-edge technology.

Babylon to Bitcoin: History of Payments

History of payments is closely entangled with the history of money, which has been prevalent since 9000 BC, or even more when human beings started living in groups and began farming, animal husbandry, and so on. To start with, they had a barter system as an elementary form of trading, which involved exchanging the extras that each family produced with something else that they needed. Then, some local banks were established for safeguarding valuables, allocating loans, and keeping records. Since then the banking sector has evolved manifold, sometimes because of rulers of that time and sometimes because of scholars or affluent people of the era. However, the purpose of a banking system since the days of inception has been more or less the same, and it can be broadly classified as follows:

- Issuance of currencies as per regulations of ruler or government
- Safeguarding wealth of people
- Record-keeping
- Investment
- Welfare of mankind

Come second century BCE, the Silk Road was discovered that connected the East with the West. The Silk Road trade played a significant role in the development of civilizations of Asia, Europe, and Africa and, at the same time, gave birth to international trading that was a much more complex form of local trading that had been carried out until then. Yet, at its heart, the trading system was still a careful barter system where traders exchanged commodities on the basis of demand and supply between countries and continents. For example, the black pepper produced in southern Indian state of Kerala would be exchanged with gold in international trading as recently as five hundred years back. Soon, the age-old barter system was replaced with payment in currencies in international trading mechanisms. Although this type of payment within a country is relatively simple, in the international arena it is far more complex, as there is a forex rate of currencies involved between both the countries, which are ever-fluctuating.

Have you ever wondered about the reason behind the fluctuation of forex rates? Well, following could be a few of them:

- Balance of payments of the country in the world market
- Base interest rate level of the country
- Inflation rate
- Fiscal and monetary policy
- Venture capital
- Government market intervention
- Economic strength of the country

It's worth noting that the exchange rate of USD, GBP, and INR was 1:1:1 back in 1947 when India got independence. However, this rate has increased manifold (for India) in the past seven decades because of many different factors as well as amendments in the monetary policies of governments. Hence, forex rate is a huge factor for traders to consider before buying or selling their goods in the international market.

Evolution of banks

Very recently, I had the opportunity to read *Bank 4.0,* a bestseller for bankers authored by Brett King, who is an Australian futurist, speaker, and author and is considered to be an influencer in financial services globally. In his book, he has divided the evolution of modern banking spanning the last five hundred years into four different phases or time periods. We can ignore any banking that happened beforehand.

Following is the roadmap to Bank 4.0, which shows a consistent strive to improve the quality of services for banking clients.

- **Bank 1.0 (1472–1980)**

Banking since ancient times until 1980s was a face-to-face, single channel business. Banks were private organizations, completely isolated from each other.

- **Bank 2.0 (1981–2007)**

Banking outside the premises of a bank began by introduction of ATMs and banking over the internet. Even then the services offered were minimal, and data syncing issues were still prevalent among the different channels of a bank.

- **Bank 3.0 (2008–2017)**

Multi-channel experience was introduced through telebanking, mobile banking, and banking services completely synchronized and integrated with FinTech products.

- **Bank 4.0 (2017 onwards)**

Superior banking experience was introduced (or will be introduced, where not done already) with super-fast facilities such as real-time money transfer, frictionless commerce, and instant clearing, as well as settlement with minimal human intervention or paperwork. Introduction of open banking, AI, and Blockchain has led to the creation of new business models.

It's quite interesting to note that even though some banks and FinTechs have jumped and moved ahead of others to migrate to the next phase, there are some players, both big and small, who are still working in the centenarian form of banking, i.e., Bank 1.0, Bank 2.0, or Bank 3.0.

Pain points of modern banking system

Authentication, KYC, AML, omni-channel customer service, self-service options —of the many pain points of the modern banking system, one prime issue that has always been persisted is instant payments, especially in international trading. This might seem only one issue; however, it is also associated with so many others, as follows:

- Instant settlement

- Complex handling of fluctuations in forex rates

- Handling risks in delivery against payment in international trading, and so on

Later in the book we will discuss use cases related to payments where loopholes in the current payment systems are a huge concern to today's businesses. We will discuss how using Ripple for instant funds transfer could help us overcome these inefficiencies.

Credibility of banks before and after 2007 crisis

If you browse the rise and fall of banks on Google, you would find hundreds of banking crises in documented human history. Most of these crises took place because of the lack of trust of people in banks for reasons such as flawed monetary policies devised by central banks or governments. After each such historic crisis, scholars have been compelled to make improvements by revising the loopholes in the banking and payment systems. Especially after 2007/2008, this consistent endeavour has brought about a revolution in the payment industry — Bitcoin.

Pre-Blockchain instant money transfer solutions

One might wonder if Bitcoin was the first digital solution in the world for global money transfer. The answer is no. *Table 1.1* below lists the electronic payment systems devised over the past two decades for the same purpose. However, they could not generate the level of trust in public as Bitcoin or Ripple did. This is for a very simple reason that the latter two are based on a secure Blockchain protocol where the consensus is decentralized, whereas the ones listed below were designed on central servers, which may pose problems the same way as banks did. **[1]**

2001	Korea	Electronic Banking System
2003	Chinese Taipei	ATM, FXML, FEDI
	Iceland	CBI Retail Netting System
2006	Malaysia	Instant Transfer
	South Africa	Real-Time Clearing
2007	Korea	CD/ATM
2008	Chile	Transferencias en linea
	UK	Faster Payment Service
2010	China	Internet Banking Payments
	India	Immediate Payment Service
2011	Costa Rica	Transferncia de Fondos
2012	Ecuador	Pago Directo
	Poland	Express ELIXR
	Sweden	BiR/Swish
2013	Turkey	BKM Express
2014	Denmark	Net Real-Time 24×7
	Italy	Jiffy
	Singapore	Fast & Secure Transfer

2015	Mexico	sPEI
	Switzerland	Twint
2017	Australia	New Payment Platform
	Saudi Arabia	Future Ready ACH
2018	Europe	SEPA Inst

Table 1.1 List of electronic payment systems in last two decades

Bitcoin: The end of money

Bitcoin was the first payment solution with a decentralized architecture that hit the market more than a decade back. Few surprising benefits because of which Bitcoin and many other crypto currencies immediately drew attention are as follows:

- Universally acceptable (except few countries)
- Low transaction fees
- Immunity to fraud
- Faster settlements for global transactions
- Prevention of identity theft

What criteria did Bitcoin lack for cross-border remittance?

Bitcoin, after an initial round of struggle and apprehensions, found a strong hold in the world of investment and payment. However, it has its downsides too. Bitcoin experts may come up with many more pain points but let me quote only the ones related to international money transfer and as a competitor to the existing SWIFT network (to be discussed further in Chapter 2).

- Bitcoin transactions are less time-consuming than SWIFT, yet not up to expectation. It takes almost one hour for Bitcoin transactions to be fixated on a ledger and declared as committed and risk-free.

- Scalability is a big issue in Bitcoin, and hence it is not suitable for many scenarios where massive amounts of transactions need to be carried out at a super-fast speed.

- Transactions are expensive in terms of fees — not at all suitable for micropayments.

- Prices of Bitcoin are too volatile, and many blogs have written on its "rags to riches and back again" stories.

- Bitcoin is banned in many countries, even today; hence international remittance is not feasible with them.

However, the best gift Bitcoin has given the twenty-first century world is its underlying technology, i.e., Blockchain.

Blockchain technology

Although this book is focused on Ripple and not Blockchain, it would be good to know some of the basic features of Blockchain. Ripple being a Blockchain product, it would help readers (especially those who are new to Blockchain) to understand the Ripple architecture and consensus details (explained in the next chapter). A few defining features of Blockchain are as follows:

- It's a distributed ledger or register; some may call it a special type of database, but let's say it's a register.

- It could be public or private.

- Every node in the network carries a copy of the ledger.

- There is no single point of failure and no downtime.

- Data in Blockchain is immutable, i.e., once stored it can't be altered.

- Each record in the database is known as a block that points to the previous block in the chain.

- Each new block consists of a group of transactions that are added at the end of a blockchain.

Advantages of Blockchain

One may wonder, if Blockchain is another type of database, why did we create it in the first place? Please note that Blockchain was introduced to us through Bitcoin, a crypto currency, and it was conceptualized to address the need of a digital currency, which a traditional database cannot.

- The data in a Blockchain ledger can't be altered.

- It's a highly secure database that uses public and private keys for transactions.

- The database is publicly available for everyone to validate and add transactions to.

- Being decentralized, there is no downtime in Blockchain, and hence transactions can be added anytime and from anywhere.

- It could be public or private as per the individual's business needs, and thus it is flexible.

- A Blockchain ledger is open to auditing anytime.

Since its inception, Blockchain has taken the market by storm. Using its distributed ledger technology, a new business model can be architected where different organizations can do business with each other in a secure way as the data is validated through cryptology and added to the ledger only after everyone's or a designated group's consensus. Year after year, the global investment in Blockchain technology is increasing exponentially by >80%. BigTechs such as IBM and Deloitte have predicted that by 2025–27, 10% of the global GDP will be retained on a Blockchain-powered secure ledger. Also, post the Bitcoin tsunami, many Blockchain and DLT protocols have flooded the market— Hyperledger Fabric, Hyperledger Sawtooth, R3 Corda, and Quorum to name a few. Most of these frameworks use different consensus models to validate the data before adding it to a ledger in a distributed environment.

It's interesting to note that among all the Blockchain use cases that we will discuss, 30% fall under the banking and finance domain. The data in *Figure 1.1* is the information published by Cambridge Judge Business School.

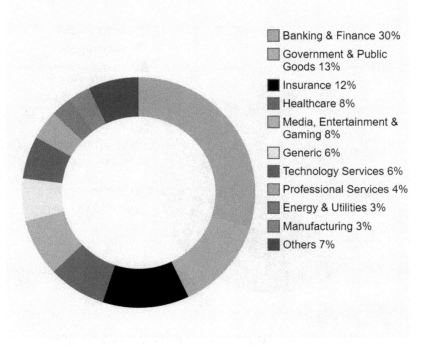

Sectors Currently Using Blockchain

- Banking & Finance 30%
- Government & Public Goods 13%
- Insurance 12%
- Healthcare 8%
- Media, Entertainment & Gaming 8%
- Generic 6%
- Technology Services 6%
- Professional Services 4%
- Energy & Utilities 3%
- Manufacturing 3%
- Others 7%

Figure 1.1: Sector-wise breakup of Blockchain use cases

Also, as shown in *Figure 1.2* below, over 40% of the Blockchain use cases involve funds transfer.

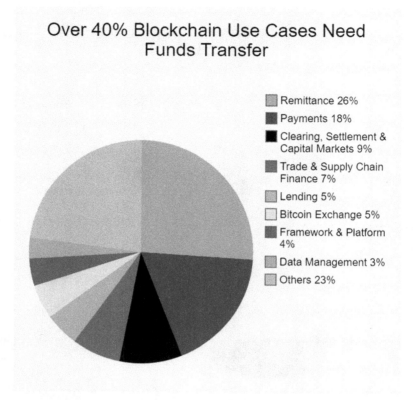

Figure 1.2: Blockchain use cases that need funds transfer

That's what makes Ripple one of the most successful and sought-after Blockchain product in the industry today, as it can be integrated with both your existing traditional application or a Blockchain-based decentralized application (will be discussed in detail in later chapters).

What is Ripple?

In 2016, Finextra reported that cross-border money transfer today is worth more than $155 trillion, and owing to factors such as changing economic trends, migration, and an increase in international commerce, this number is on an exponential rise year after year. With a market share of 95%, today banks are dominating this space, but their money transfer systems suffer because of lack of transparency, high fees, and huge delays. This area had remained untouched for ages, but lately FinTechs, with the help of cutting-edge technologies, have started working on eliminating international trading friction and providing innovative and customer-centric services to consumers and businesses. The leader in this space today is Ripple.

Ripple is a private FinTech organization that targeted this $155 remittance industry and has achieved overwhelming success in an extremely short span of time. Ripple was founded by Chris Larsen and Jed McCaleb in 2012, who came up with a payment and exchange network (RippleNet) on top of a distributed ledger database (XRP Ledger). The main goal of Ripple was to create a network for banks, payment providers, and digital asset exchanges to transfer money globally by enabling faster and cost-efficient payments across the world. However, it was conceptualized long back.

In 2004, Ryan Fugger, a decentralized systems developer, conceptualized Ripple and developed the first prototype as a decentralized digital monetary system (RipplePay) that went live in 2005 and was meant to provide secure payment solutions within a global network.

In 2012, Fugger sold this innovative solution to Jed McCaleb and Chris Larsen, and together they built a new FinTech start-up in USA, called OpenCoin, which was rebranded to Ripple Labs in 2013 and again rebranded to Ripple in 2015. By that time, Bitcoin was already popular in the market, and thus, armed with the knowledge of the pros and cons of Bitcoin, Ripple deployed the **Ripple Consensus Ledger (RCL)** in 2012 along with its native crypto currency XRP. Later Ripple renamed the ledger to **XRP Ledger (XRPL)**.

Bitcoin uses a consensus model called *Proof of Work* that is slow, resource intensive, and expensive. This model would not suit a payment network. Hence, Ripple came up with a different consensus model to validate and add new data to the network. We will discuss the consensus model of Ripple's XRP Ledger in Chapter 2 in detail. As per Ripple's website, XRPL is completely open source, and hence anyone can contribute to making it a better product by adding more features to it.

- **Performance**

Ripple is a super-fast global network for payment processing where funds can get transferred in less than four seconds. This is far less than any other Blockchain product such as Bitcoin (takes an hour), Ethereum (minutes), and the good old SWIFT network (which takes days together).

- **Scalability**

As per latest information on Ripple's website, "XRP consistently handles 1,500 **transactions per second (TPS)**, 24[×]7, and can scale to handle the same throughput as Visa" against 15 TPS by Ethereum or 3–6 TPS on the Bitcoin network.

- **Fees**

The transaction fees spent on the Ripple network are almost negligible. We will discuss this feature at length in later chapters and explain why it is favourable for micropayment business models.

XRP

Just like Bitcoin and Ether, XRP is a crypto currency. Ripple is not the founder or creator of XRP; rather 100 billion XRPs were created before Ripple was formed. XRP was introduced to the market in 2012 with a 100 billion supply, out of which 20 billion XRPs were retained by the creators and the rest 80% were gifted to Ripple (then OpenCoin, Inc). Today Ripple owns most of those XRPs (~60%) and utilizes them for international payments to go with its payment platform, RippleNet. However, 55 billion of these XRP tokens are safely locked up in an escrow account, to *create certainty of XRP supply at any given time.* Hence, only a handful of all the currencies are in circulation, according to Ripple.

As of June 2019, XRP is the third most valuable crypto currency with a market capitalization of $17.1 billion. *Figure 1.3* below shows a screenshot taken from https://coinmarketcap.com/. Each coin can be bought for ~$0.4 as of July 2019.

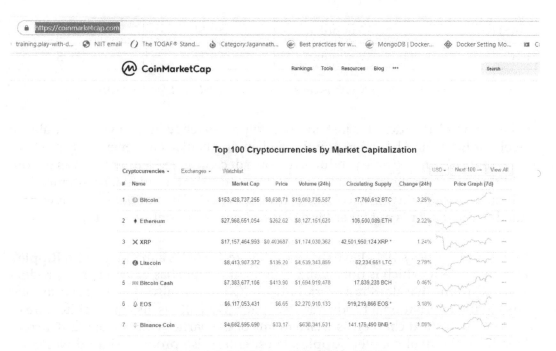

Figure 1.3: Market capitalization of XRP

Although both Bitcoin (or other crypto currencies) and Ripple/XRP are crypto currencies, they belong to two entirely different categories of products. They are conceptualized to handle different use cases. Bitcoin and other crypto currencies are digital currencies that work on a distributed decentralized platform. XRP, on the other hand, is meant for real-time money transfer in a cheaper, faster, more efficient way. One may wonder, faster, cheaper, and efficient, but how much? *Table 1.2* below compares a few parameters of XRP against some of its contemporaries. The data was published by **coin5s.com** and https://cryptocurrencynews.com/daily-news/ripple-news/ripple-looks-unstoppable-xcurrent-xrapid/ claiming XRP to be the *best digital asset for payments*.

[handwritten: XRP's Purpose vs Bitcoin's]

	Speed	Cost	Scalability
XRP	3 seconds	$0.0004	1500 TPS
BTC	66 minutes	$28.23	32 TPS
ETH	2 minutes	$0.96	16 TPS
BCH	58 minutes	$0.26	64 TPS

| DASH | 15 minutes | $0.64 | 10 TPS |
| LTC | 17 minutes | $0.37 | 56 TPS |

Table 1.2 Why Ripple is considered best digital asset for payments

As per some XRP critics, it is just another crypto currency in the market, similar to Bitcoin or Ether, and has been popularized among banks. However, they must not forget that although Ripple products run on a decentralized ledger (such as Bitcoin and Ethereum), it's customized to match the needs of international remittance (i.e., high speed, scalability, low cost, and transparency). The validation of new data added to the ledger is not taken care of by all nodes but only a select few.

Many Ripple critics still believe that working with XRP is a mandate with Ripple's payment system, which is not a valid statement. Ripple has an enterprise product called xCurrent that does not work only on XRP but is also very popular among banks in the international funds transfer space. We will discuss the architecture of xCurrent in the next chapter, as well as some of the parties who are using xCurrent globally, in the final chapter. Ripple's latest enterprise product xRapid works on XRP and is gaining popularity among more and more people lately.

Advantages of Ripple

One may wonder why Ripple Labs, a small organization founded in 2012 and with just ~150 employees to date, has taken the global payment industry by storm. Following are some of the advantages that our thousand-year-old banking system never offered.

- Transfer of funds between domestic as well as cross-border banks is completed in real time, i.e., in under four seconds, in comparison to SWIFT gpi, which achieves the same in close to thirty minutes.

- Fees for transactions are nominal. The current minimum transaction cost as advised by the network for a standard transaction is 0.00001 XRP (10 drops) in comparison to a whopping $25 for each wire transfer over SWIFT.

- Ripple eliminates the need for *nostro and vostro accounts*, which block a fortune to minimize the risk related to the delay in liquidity when transferring funds from one account to another.

- Ripple works with most of the fiat and crypto currencies for money transfer.

Each of these points will be further explained with examples in later chapters.

Disadvantages of Ripple

Ripple comes with its own drawbacks as well, and business leaders should know them before investing in this space. Some are listed as follows:

- Being a crypto currency, Ripple is not backed by any collateral or guarantee.

- Price of XRP, which is one part of Ripple's main business, is ever fluctuating.

- Ripple may have regulation issues in certain countries where crypto currencies are banned.

- Ripple is not understood in many different parts of the world, and hence it's an additional job to educate the masses.

Why are banks still hesitant to adopt Ripple?

Banks in general are risk-averse and resistant towards adoption of cutting-edge technologies. However, in case of Ripple, this myth is not true. In the concluding chapter, we will explore some of the biggest banks of the world and their flirtation with Ripple.

Misconceptions and unknown facts of Ripple

There are many misconceptions and unknown facts regarding Ripple that discourage funders from investing money in Ripple and XRP. Following are a few of them:

- **Misconception: Ripple is XRP, and XRP is Ripple.**

    o Ripple is a privately owned organization that deals with a real-time gross settlement system. For doing so, it uses XRP as a digital asset to transfer value on its XRP Ledger, a global ledger that lets us transfer funds between any two places in the world.

- **Misconception: XRP is infinite.**

  o Just like Bitcoin, the native crypto currency XRP is finite in supply with its total circulation value of 100 billion XRP.

- **Misconception: XRP can be mined.**

  o Unlike most of the regular crypto currencies such as Bitcoin or Ether, XRP cannot be mined. Against every transaction, a part of XRP is burnt, or just gets wasted, but it does not go to the miners. The sole purpose of this process is to discourage malicious users from spamming the network. In total, 100 billion XRPs are in circulation. Hence, there is no issue of consensus or other related hassles such as wastage of energy or any other consensus mechanism.

  gets wasted?

- **Misconception: XRP is a non-starter.**

  o As of June 2019, PNC Bank, Santander Bank, MoneyGram, Mercury FX, IDT, Cuallix, Western Union, Cambridge Global Payments, Currencies Direct, and Viamericas — some big names in the banking and payment industry — have publicly announced their interest in Ripple products. All of them are investing money, efforts, and time on pilot programs using XRP in payment flows through xRapid to provide frictionless liquidity solutions for their cross-border payments. [2]

- **Misconception: XRP lacks security.**

  o XRP transactions are performed on XRP Ledger, a distributed ledger where data validation is done by many. Hence, it's as secure as any other safe system for holding and transferring money.

- **Misconception: XRP Ledger is centralized in control.**

  o In XRP Ledger consensus, the process of addition of new data to a ledger is slightly different from Bitcoin. Not all but a selected group or a subset of all the nodes participates in the validation process, which makes it faster and reliable at the same time. However, it's certainly not centralized in control as some people believe.

- **Misconception: Ripple has hidden cost.**

  o Ripple has no hidden cost except the fee that the user pays to XRP Ledger during money transfer. This amount, with a minimum value of 0.00001 XRP, determines how soon the transaction will be executed post validation by validators. Unlike Bitcoin, part of this transaction fee is burnt, not paid to the validator. This makes XRP a deflationary currency, and protects the network against spam attacks.

  [handwritten note: ✳ Deflationary Currency]

- **Misconception: XRP's price and supply are controlled by Ripple.**

  o Although Ripple holds large amount of XRPs, it has little control on its price, which goes up or down as per the demand and supply in the market, just like most other crypto currencies.

- **Misconception: XRP price is too volatile, and hence unsuitable for business.**

  o During one of my sessions in Philadelphia earlier this year, someone from the audience asked me this question. He even showed me the spot price of XRP against the highest and lowest price of XRP that day. *Figure 1.4* below is a screenshot from https://www.coingecko.com/en/coins/ripple that shows the price fluctuation of USD/XRP in just twenty-four hours.

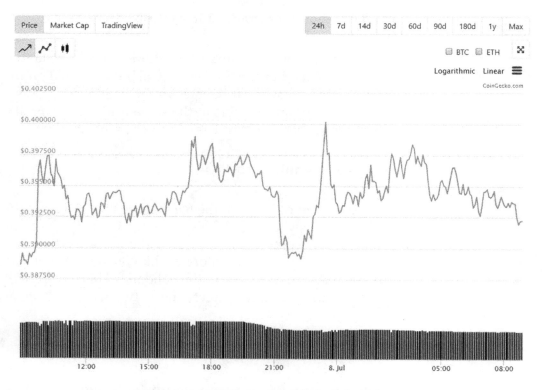

Figure 1.4: Price fluctuation of Ripple in 24 hours

Please note that in any real-time business where we need instant money transfer (domestic or international) or instant settlement feature, we find out the spot price of USD/XRP and transfer the equivalent amount of XRPs to the payee's account where it is converted back to USD or any other currency. This money transfer using XRP happens in about four seconds. Hence, price fluctuation really does not affect the business.

- **Misconception: SWIFT and Ripple are working together.**

    o   As of now, they are competitors. In fact, recently, SWIFT announced its interest in adopting Blockchain, especially R3 Corda.

- **Misconception: Banks are threatened by Ripple.**

    o   Not at all; in fact, in the final chapter we will discuss how many banks globally are adopting different Ripple products.

FinTechs on XRP ecosystem

As per Ripple's Q1 report for 2019, RippleNet has more than two hundred financial institutions as clients worldwide and Ripple's native currency XRP is listed on approximately 120 exchanges worldwide. You can refer to XRPArcade https://www.xrparcade.com/xrpecosystem/ to find an ever-growing long list of FinTechs who are already using or have plans to use XRP in future. The list could be much bigger as not all organizations make it public until they are in production.

Ripple/XRP versus Stellar/XLM

The only other player in the crypto currency market with a similar goal as Ripple (i.e., cut downtime cost and improve efficiency of international remittance) is Stellar. Just like the Ripple and XRP alliance, Stellar comes with its own distributed ledger to facilitate fast and low-cost cross-border transactions with the help of its own native currency, Lumens (XLM). Some of the points of comparison between these two products are as follows:

- Ripple is in operation since early 2012, whereas Stellar hit the market in 2014.

- Stellar is inflationary, whereas Ripple is not.

- Stellar takes two to five seconds for processing a transaction, whereas Ripple claims it does so in less than four seconds.

- Stellar is far less popular and market adoption is much less than that of Ripple today.

- Stellar currently is targeting a market for individuals, whereas Ripple is doing so for financial institutions.

As we are discussing operation of banks and FinTechs here, a discussion of Stellar is beyond the scope of this book.

Summary

In this chapter, we covered the following topics:

- The history of banking and payments, and their loopholes

- The basics of Bitcoin and Blockchain technology

- What led to the invention of Ripple

- The differentiators of Ripple against its contemporaries

Questions

1. What is the relationship between Ripple and XRP?

    A. They are two different organizations with no link up.

    B. Ripple is the founder and owner of XRP crypto currency.

    C. Ripple and XRP are different organizations. Ripple uses XRP as its native crypto currency.

2. Which issue in international remittance is Ripple trying to solve?

    A. International remittance is expensive.

    B. International remittance is slow.

    C. International remittance lacks transparency.

    D. All of the above

3. How much time does Ripple take to complete an international transaction?

    A. Around two to five days

    B. Maximum one day

    C. Few minutes

    D. Under four seconds

4. Which are the top three crypto currencies in terms of market cap?

    A. Bitcoin, Ripple, Ethereum

    B. Bitcoin, EOS, Litecoin

    C. Bitcoin, Ethereum, EOS

    D. Bitcoin, Ether, XRP

5. What is the minimum fee that XRP Ledger charges for a transaction?

   A. It's free of cost.

   B. 10 USD

   C. 10 XRP

   D. 10 drops where 1 drop = 0.000001 XRP

6. How scalable is XRP on Ripple network?

   A. 100 TPS

   B. 500 TPS

   C. 1000 TPS

   D. 1500 TPS

7. Who, at the moment, is a close competitor to Ripple as the future of cross-border payment?

   A. Bitcoin

   B. USD

   C. Libra

   D. Stellar

8. What are the different products offered by Ripple?

   A. xVia

   B. xCurrent

   C. xRapid

   D. All of the above

Answers

1 C, 2 D, 3 D, 4 D, 5 D, 6 D, 7 D, 8 D

References

1. Ripple versus JPM Coin. Real competition? - https://cryptonomist.ch/en/2019/02/20/ripple-vs-jpm-coin-2/

2. The Biggest Banks Using Ripple Products - https://usethebitcoin.com/the-biggest-banks-using-ripple-products/

Some other great resources for reference are as follows:

1. What is Ripple - https://www.binance.vision/economics/what-is-ripple

2. The Future of Cross-Border Payments: Ripple and Co. - https://www.financemagnates.com/fintech/payments/the-future-of-cross-border-payments-ripple-and-co/

3. A Brief(ish) History Of XRP - https://medium.com/coinmonks/a-brief-ish-history-of-xrp-6fb434a35208

CHAPTER 2

Ripple Architecture

In this chapter, we will touch upon the current pain points of **Society for Worldwide Interbank Financial Telecommunication (SWIFT)**, the existing international remittance network, and how Ripple has come up to bridge that gap with its innovative solution. We will then move on to the overall architecture of Ripple, learn all the products that Ripple offers, and understand how they can benefit international financial transactions and open up opportunities for new models of business.

How does international remittance work?

Transferring money from one bank to another where the two are in different countries is called international remittance or international money transfer. Money, as I have explained in Chapter 1, is a medium of exchange of value when procuring products and services. Probably money is one of the greatest inventions in human history, and over the last thousand years, international money transfer has remained an integral part of trading between states and countries. Today, there are a number of service providers for international remittance, such as Western Union, WorldRemit, XE Money Transfer, TransferWise, Travelex, MoneyGram, or PayPal; yet international remittance has remained one of the pain points in business transactions owing to high processing time, or high cost of transaction, or low transparency of transaction, or all.

Before discussing the issues in international remittance in detail, let's take baby steps in understanding how money transfer works among banks at different levels in today's world.

Intrabank money transfer

In intrabank money transfer, the money does not leave the parent bank; rather it's deducted from one account and added to another on the bank's ledger as shown in *Figure 2.1*:

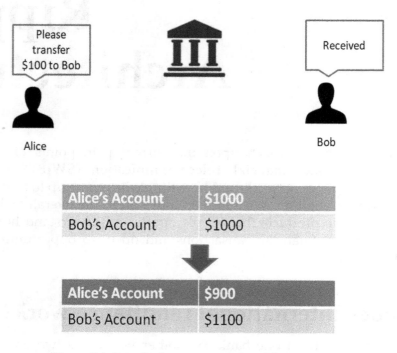

Figure 2.1: Intrabank money transfer within country

As a result, we can do it at our own beck and call. No wonder the transfer at times happens within a second if not less, and it's a perfect synchronous process in most banks across the world.

Interbank money transfer

If the money has to be transferred between two different banks within the same country, then we need the help of an intermediary bank called *the central bank*, which works in close association with the government of the nation. As shown in *Figure 2.2* below, both the banks would have accounts with the central bank.

So, for each transaction, internally there is more than one transaction happening. Money is deducted from the first bank and then the central bank is informed, where account of Bank 1 is deducted, and Bank 2 is updated with the additional money. Now, Bank 2 will add that amount to the right receiver's account.

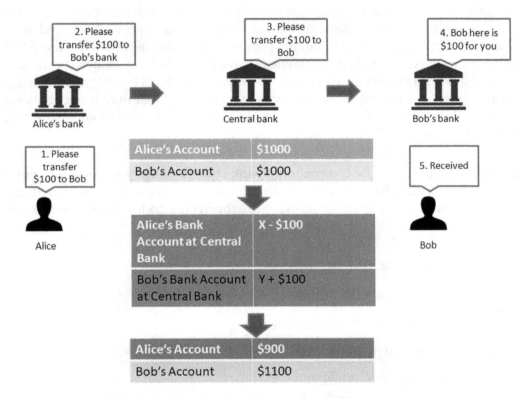

Figure 2.2: Interbank money transfers within country

So, the clearing process takes some time, and both the sender and receiver in most cases are informed by text or email of the success or failure of the transaction.

International money transfer

International money transfer is pretty much similar to interbank money transfer; however, there is no central bank or a central server. Instead, there are international money payment networks such as SWIFT and SEPA, which function in a similar way. Let's explore their business model.

SWIFT

SWIFT is the biggest payment and settlement network connecting close to eleven thousand banks across two hundred countries and territories in the world, and it has been in operation for the past forty-six years. SWIFT's services are used globally by numerous banks, securities dealers, asset management companies, exchanges, depositories, clearing houses, foreign exchange brokers, and so on. Everyday approximately 24 million messages are transferred over the SWIFT network. Its services, even if not flawless, have generated unparalleled trust in the world banking network in the last four to five decades. This might be a reason, good enough, for not introducing any new technology that may bring challenges to the healthy bread and butter business of SWIFT. Let's explore some of the basics of the SWIFT system.

SWIFT allocates a unique international bank code to identify a particular bank in the whole world. A bank that is not allocated a SWIFT code cannot participate in international money transfer. Following are the SWIFT codes of a few well-known banks.

- Bank of China: BKCHCNBJ

- Deutsche Bank: DEUTDEBB

- JPMorgan Chase Bank: CHASUS33

- ICICI Bank: ICICINBB

- NatWest Bank: NWBKGB2L

SWIFT also comes with the following SWIFT currency codes:

- USD (US Dollar)

- GBP (Great Britain Pound)

- EUR (Euro)

- INR (Indian Rupee)

These currency codes are used internationally for representing the different fiat currencies. Now, let's explore how money transfer works over SWIFT. As shown in *Figure 2.3* below, the SWIFT framework works on a messaging model. Rather than sending money, it just sends messages to banks who directly or indirectly are involved in the transaction.

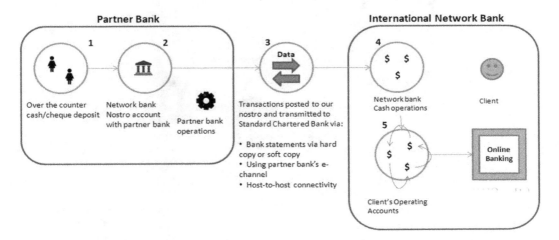

Figure 2.3: Message transfer on SWIFT network

In the SWIFT model, most of the banks have a commercial account (called nostro and vostro accounts) of other banks on their system. They only update the amount in their commercial account in different countries as per requirement.

Here is a scenario where Alice in New York wants to send $1000 from Bank of America to Bob in Japan having an account in Japanese Bank. Let's imagine that Bank of America and Japanese Bank do not have a direct connection, i.e., they do not have each other's account. Hence, they would take the help of an intermediary bank, i.e., NatWest Bank in the UK, which has both their accounts.

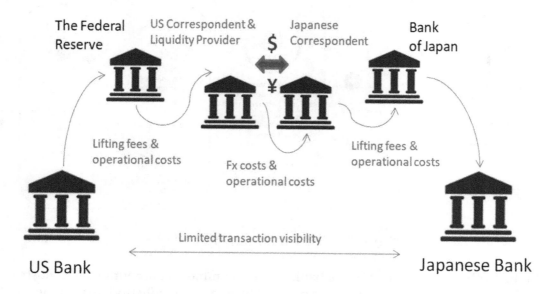

Figure 2.4: With SWIFT settlement, international funds transfer may take up to three days. Source Ripple Labs white paper titled "The cost cutting case of banks".

A message is sent from Bank of America to NatWest bank on the transaction, and money is transferred in NatWest Bank's US local commercial account.

NatWest bank will deduct a small amount of fees for the transaction and will transfer the rest of the amount to Japanese Bank in Japan by updating the commercial accounts of both the banks.

Japanese Bank will finally update Bob's personal account with the money, which would be ($1000, fees levied by intermediary bank as currency conversion charges) converted to Japanese Yen.

SWIFT pain points

Let's discuss some of the pain points of the SWIFT system that has been here since decades.

- SWIFT payments usually take one to three days. However, depending upon the time difference between two countries, country-specific regulations, banking holidays, and number of hops the transaction requires, it might take more time, i.e., up to five working days.

- Also, each bank in the entire transfer charges some transferring fee and currency conversion fees, to add to the load. Hence, more the number of hops, more would be the final cost of money transfer.

- Cost of transaction is too high on SWIFT, thus barring micro-funding platforms from working in the global space with the SWIFT network.

Introduction of SWIFT global payment innovation (gpi)

In order to find a frictionless global payment solution and also to survive in the market after the introduction of Ripple, in early 2017 SWIFT introduced SWIFT gpi, a product that has found many happy banking customers so far. As per SWIFT, "SWIFT gpi is a quantum leap to improve speed, security and transparency issues in payment processing standards which is now being used by 165 member banks." SWIFT achieves this by introducing the following features:

1. gpi tracker: End-to-end tracking of processing of payments is done.

2. gpi observer: The observer keeps an eye if the members are adhering to the SLA rules during remittance.

3. gpi directory: It provides a list of all the gpi members and banks.

As per Finextra news report in December 2018, "During 2018, SWIFT's gpi payments service continued to radically transform correspondent banking. With the support of hundreds of financial institutions, including the world's 60 biggest banks, it is now being used to send hundreds of billions in payments every day – more than half (55%) of SWIFT's cross-border traffic."

While introduction of SWIFT gpi could bring down the international money transfer from days to minutes, as per many it's just old wine in a new bottle as there is no serious alteration of technology. Perhaps the sole reason behind the introduction of gpi was its close competition with Ripple. But the temporary advantage that SWIFT has over Ripple is its far wider network, banking clients' reluctance to adopt new technology, and their least appetite for risk.

However, the trouble with SWIFT does not end here. Their bigger issue is with nostro accounts; let's find out how.

Liquidity issue with nostro accounts

Nostro and vostro are words used to describe a bank's commercial account, as discussed before. They are two sides of the same coin, i.e., the same account could be termed as nostro or vostro with respect to the owner.

As shown in *Figure 2.5* below, let's consider we are sending an amount from Bank A to Bank C using an intermediary Bank B: Bank A (USA) -> Bank B (Europe) -> Bank C (Japan).

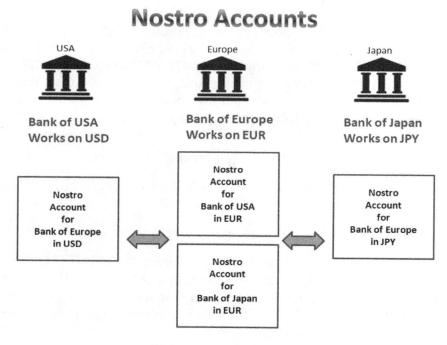

Figure 2.5: Nostro accounts

In this case, Bank A terms its commercial account with intermediary Bank B as a nostro account. Nostro in banking world means *ours*. The same account is a vostro account for Bank B where Vostro means *yours*. This one account handles all its client's remittance requirements by getting added or deducted.

International money transfers experience a significant delay in time and suffer because of fluctuations in forex rates of the involved currencies. That's why most banks reserve money in local currencies in their nostro accounts to improve liquidity and match any risk involved with currencies and price fluctuations. This feature, however, costs them a fortune.

A 2016 report by McKinsey Global Payments claims that around $5 trillion are reserved totally idle in nostro and vostro accounts.

Not all banks have that kind of money to facilitate international money transfer by having enough liquidity; only a handful do. The rest just pay an additional fee to avail services from their larger bank counterparts.

Ripple: The new-age payment system

Most people believe that with Ripple, adoption of the crypto currency XRP becomes mandatory, which is not true. Please note that Ripple and XRP are separate entities, and XRP is not used in all of Ripple's products. Now, let's review Ripple's products and their features.

XRP Ledger

At the heart of Ripple's base product RippleNet lies XRP Ledger, a Blockchain-powered peer-to-peer network of servers where each node is a participating individual or organization. XRP Ledger by default uses XRP, a crypto currency used as a digital token to exchange fiat and crypto currencies as well as valuables, and facilitates frictionless money transfer globally in almost no time at a much less price by eliminating all third-party costs.

Consensus in XRP Ledger

The consensus is a special mechanism in a distributed system to validate new data from any of the nodes before adding them to the ledger. In a centralized server it's not a big deal, as the central server is the final decision maker who has access to the database or ledger that has just one version running at any point of time. However, in a distributed environment, there would be many nodes and each bearing a copy of the ledger whose versions might be different from each other. Hence, keeping all of them in sync and at the same time validating data so that fraudulence is in check, as well as regular data validation, could be a pretty complex process. In

Bitcoin, every node can participate in the validation process, which is called **Proof of Work (PoW)**. However, PoW is time-consuming and resource intensive, which would not be appropriate for payment protocols such as Ripple.

Many people believe that the validation and consensus process in Ripple is centralized, which is not true at all. Ripple runs on a special algorithm called **Ripple protocol consensus algorithm (RPCA)** that is applied on the network every few seconds and runs in rounds. Each node in the Ripple network is a server that chooses a subset of the entire network as that server's trusted validators, or **unique node list (UNL)**. Hence, each node's UNL might be different. Any new transactional data added by a node would be validated by the nodes in its UNL. Now let's discuss the life cycle of a transaction.

- Validator nodes usually start from a previously validated XRP ledger where all transactions are valid and committed to the ledger after rounds of desirable consensus.

- A new transaction is signed by a secret key and sent by the client (owner of XRP account) and is submitted to the network.

- All the transactions are collected for this round and sorted in a canonical order in which all servers would process them so that the validation order would remain the same for all. The canonical order is determined using an algorithm based on account number, sequence number, and transaction ID.

- These new lists of transactions are broadcast to the network and can be validated by all; however, only the ones accepted and approved by UNL nodes are considered to be final.

- Unlike Bitcoin where consensus is achieved at just above 50%, in Ripple network transactions are committed to a ledger only after more than 80% UNL nodes find them agreeable.

- After all transactions in that account are applied to the ledger, it's considered a *closed ledger*.

- The ledger version goes up by one.

- On the other hand, during the process of ongoing consensuses, the ledger is called an *open ledger* that is working towards next version of the ledger.

Rippled Server

As already discussed, XRP Ledger consists of a huge number of nodes, where each node is known as a rippled server. However not all of them are validating nodes.

A rippled server can be of three types:

- Stock server: It follows the network with a local copy of the ledger.

- Validating server/Validator: It can do everything that a stock server does, and also participates in the consensus process.

- Stand-alone mode: It is used just for testing. It cannot communicate with other rippled servers.

You can run one or more of the above servers for your own use. The stand-alone server can be used for signing or validating a transaction before submitting it to the network of rippled servers.

If several transactions are needed for your business with significant money transfer, you can go for the stock server so that you can participate in the show directly without depending on others to decide when and how you can access it.

You can run a validating server by keeping it on a private network and a stock server on a public network, and then you can give access to the validating server only through the stock server, which gives you better security and control as well as tough resistance to those trying to compromise the integrity of your validating server. You can learn more on how to run either of them here: https://xrpl.org/rippled-server-modes.html.

XRP

The much talked about and third most popular crypto currency in the world as per market capitalization is XRP, which is also the native currency of XRP Ledger. Most functionalities of the ledger, such as direct payment, checks, escrow, partial payment, or payment channels, will be discussed in Chapter 3. While working with XRP, for any of these features one must find out that day's forex rate with their own country's local currency (https://min-api.cryptocompare.com/data/pricehistorical?fsym=USD&tsyms=XRP). If your business is in need of international remittance, then the fiat currency can be converted to XRP at one end and the XRP can again be converted to any other currency in another country. The whole process takes around four seconds. The price fluctuation of XRP would be minimal and transaction fees are negligible on XRP Ledger. Hence, working with XRPs is close to risk-free under such scenarios, especially in international remittance and trading where money transfer is painful for its sky-high fees and endless waiting time.

Drops

The lowest fraction of XRP is known as drop, whose value is 0.000001 XRP. It makes payment in XRP in the least amount possible and can support the micropayment industry, i.e., the lowest amount that can be transferred on the ledger can go as little as 0.000001 XRP. The minimum fees per transaction on XRP Ledger are 10 drops.

Issued currencies

All the non-XRP currencies that XRP Ledger supports are called *issued currencies* (also known as *issuances* or *IOUs*). Issued currencies are represented on XRP Ledger with a three-character international currency code such as USD. For fiat currencies, all three-character currency codes can be found on https://www.xe.com/iso4217. php. Funds in issued currencies can be transferred from one account to another if both of them operate on the same currency code.

Trust lines

The issued currencies are similar to **I owe you** (**IOU**) or a signed document acknowledging a debt based on fiat currencies that are represented on XRP Ledger with a placeholder. However, who would give a guarantee for their reserve outside the ledger? For doing so, we need trust lines that are a way to represent how much you trust an issuer to hold on your behalf. We can set different limits for issued currencies to different trust lines to indicate the maximum amount we are willing to let the issuer *owe* us in XRP Ledger. The risk involved would be the amount of money that is on the trust line and might get lost if the trust line absconds or goes out of business. It's significant to note that each trust line operates on a specific currency code.

Freezing issued currencies

One of the super-cool features of issued currencies is the ledger's power to *freeze* or restrict movement of currencies in the accounts. This could be highly beneficial in some business functions of delivery against payment, where the currency can be held for some time period using this feature for the peace of mind of the participating parties.

The freeze function can be set up on an individual basis where two parties enter into this deal. Especially in a delivery against payment scenario, the seller may demand the buyer to freeze a certain amount for payment. Here the amount can be only sent to the seller and no one else. This is especially beneficial where the seller does not trust the buyer who has an unscrupulous credit history.

Similarly, we can set up a global freeze between one party and all its counterparties. In that case also, all counterparties can send funds to only the former party.

A *no freeze* feature can also be set on accounts when no obligation of fund freezing is needed.

Note that XRP cannot be represented as an issued currency, and hence it cannot be used for freezing funds.

RippleNet

RippleNet is Ripple's global payment network that is used by more than two hundred banks and payment providers worldwide today, some of which we will discuss in the final chapter. Using RippleNet, customers can transfer funds to any other user on the network in seconds at a low fee and with high visibility and transparency. Ripple offers three products for international money transfer: xVia, xCurrent, and xRapid.

As per Abhay Salitri, Head of Financial Institutions Business at InstaReM, "RippleNet provides a single platform to quickly introduce new corridors, offer lower fees and faster transaction times — all while reducing operational overhead. Our customers now have low-cost, traceable payment services in and out of more than 55 countries worldwide."

Please note that RippleNet is a Ripple product that is built on XRP Ledger and used as a payment and exchange network. But how would you join the RippleNet network? Well, you have two choices: xVia and xCurrent.

xVia (standard access)

xVia is the standard payment interface for joining the RippleNet network, and it comes with all the default features of Ripple we just discussed. With xVia, one does not need to install any additional software and banks can start trying xVia as the first step for sending money globally.

xVia, as shown in *Figure 2.6* below, works on a bi-directional messaging protocol over the Ripple network to confirm forex rates and fees before commencing an actual transfer of funds. The figure explains the direction of fund flow as well as bi-directional messaging between the payment provider, receiving correspondent, and beneficiary bank.

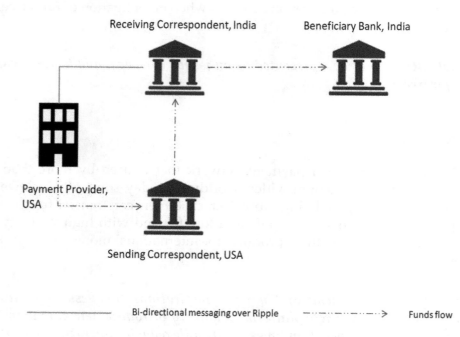

Figure 2.6: Working model of xVia. Pic source: https://www.coindesk.com/xrp-fits-ripples-payments-products-explained

Using xVia, one can pay in local currency or XRP, track payments, and generate invoice.

With xVia, it's not mandatory to use Ripple's native currency XRP, although it's an option.

xCurrent (full access)

xCurrent is the enterprise international remittance solution from Ripple, and it is their most popular product in the market, used by many major banks in the world. Using xCurrent, banks can transfer funds to different currencies as per the current forex rate.

As per Stefan Thomas, CTO Ripple, "It provides a single source of truth for the transacting counterparties while preserving the privacy of banking customers' identifiable payment information."

It's noteworthy that, as shown in *Figure 2.7* below, xCurrent is not built on XRP Ledger and also does not use Ripple's default crypto currency XRP. Rather, it's built on top of the **Interledger Protocol** (**ILP**), which is another platform designed and built by Ripple as a protocol for connecting different ledgers or payment networks.

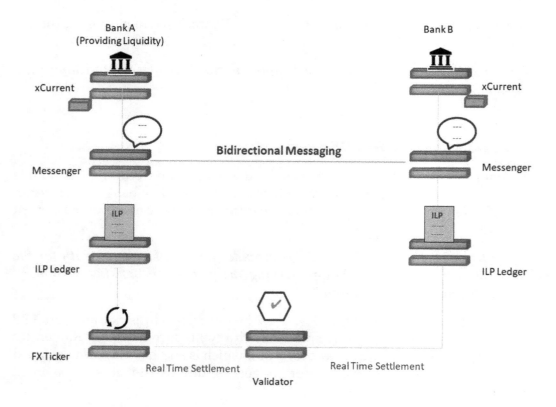

Figure 2.7: Working model of xCurrent with Messenger, Validator, ILP ledger, and FX Ticker. Picture source: https://ripple.com/files/ripple_solutions_guide.pdf

The four building blocks of xCurrent are as follows:

1. **Messenger**: Messengers can be used to retrieve all the vital information regarding a transaction (forex, fees, associated risks, expected time of completion of transaction, etc.) before the transaction begins. It's possible to connect financial institutions on a peer-to-peer basis and track the payment until it's delivered.

2. **Validator**: International transactions between financial organizations involve large chunks of money transfer. Validators are introduced to evaluate the success or failure of transactions by tracking the movement of funds over the Interledger. While many big financial organizations can build their own validator, one has the option of going with a third-party validator on the network.

3. **ILP Ledger**: ILP Ledger is the ledger for tracking credits, debits, and liquidity across participating financial organizations. They work in close association with the ledgers of the banks to collect such information. They help to settle funds transfer instantly by securing the atomicity of the transaction.

4. **FX Ticker**: FX ticker is mainly used to determine the forex rates before the transaction.

xCurrent can be used both with fiat currencies and crypto currencies in transactions.

Figure 2.8 shows how xCurrent be used with XRP for best possibilities.

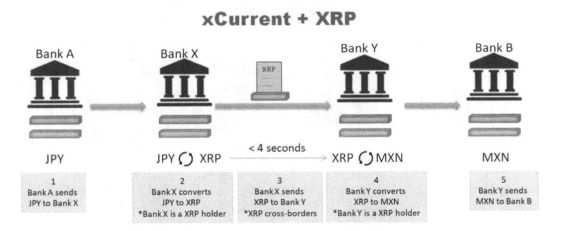

Figure 2.8: Working model of xCurrent with XRP. Picture source:
https://twitter.com/XRPTrump/status/1063093085570101248

Today xCurrent is not managed by Ripple anymore, but it's with a **World Wide Web Consortium (W3C)** group, run by a long-standing non-profit organization dedicated to furthering internet standard. The main goal of this project is the provision of interoperability between all fiat and non-fiat currencies, not just crypto currencies. Hence, parties who still doubt or are unwilling to work with XRP can stay happy with xCurrent at the moment for their international remittance.

xRapid

Based on its native crypto currency XRP, xRapid is the liquidity solution from Ripple. We have already discussed how international remittance has always been slow owing to the absence of a direct relationship between certain banks. In that case, we introduce intermediary banks for the entire flow of money. Each bank, whosoever is involved in the money transfer, charges its fees, which makes it an extremely expensive affair. To handle this issue, Ripple uses XRP to do the conversion of currencies instantly.

In short, xRapid uses both XRP and XRP Ledger, which enables faster confirmation times and much lower fees when compared to conventional methods. In *Figure 2.9* below, you can see how xRapid converts fiat and crypto currencies to XRP at one end of the world, does the funds transfer at lightning speed, and transfers them back to the desired currencies at the other end.

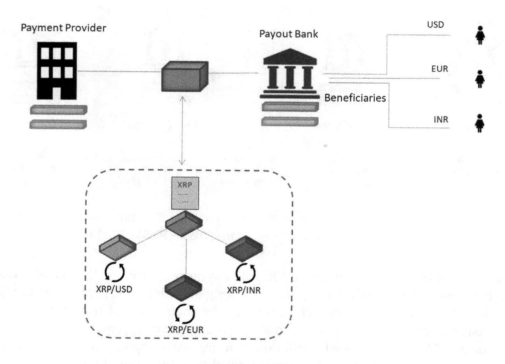

Figure 2.9: Working model of xRapid. Picture
Source: https://ripple.com/ripplenet/source-liquidity/

International payment giant MoneyGram is currently testing xRapid on its platform. So let's consider the following situation with MoneyGram (in a futuristic context).

Alice in New York wishes to send $1000 to Bob in London and reaches out to MoneyGram. So, MoneyGram would convert $1000 to XRP as per the forex rate of that date at one end and convert XRPs to GBP at the other end using xRapid. Bob can withdraw the money from MoneyGram's asset exchange located in London.

Figure 2.10 shows how xRapid can be used with xCurrent for best possibilities.

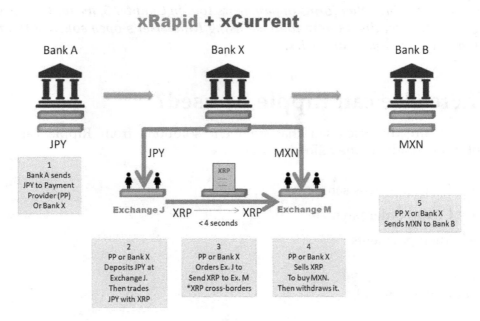

Figure 2.10: Working model of xRapid and xCurrent together. Picture source:
https://twitter.com/XRPTrump/status/1063093085570101248

xCurrent 4.0

On March 6, 2019, Ripple's CTP David Schwartz tweeted: "4.0 is live. We're working to get all customers upgraded, but it's a complex process. Multihop, xRapid support, much easier peering, and a much easier customer integration process are the major new features."

xCurrent 4.0 is Ripple's offer for their 200+ customer base to upgrade their xCurrent platform. Just like xCurrent, this new version xCurrent 4.0 is an enterprise solution for financial institutions. Banks can use it to communicate and carry out cross-border payments with end-to-end transaction tracking and payment confirmation with transaction details. xRapid will be a blessing for merchants, for it is a payment service that allows them to use XRP tokens to request liquidity and make payments in real time using any fiat or crypto currency as per the need. This would significantly reduce the costs of accepting crypto currencies or payments in general.

Using RippleNet does not necessarily mean using only XRP for money transfer; you can do it using other forms of payments too. In Chapter 3, we will discuss the programmatic details on how to do so using RippleNet's open source APIs with XRP as well as issued currencies.

Where else can Ripple be used?

We have already discussed that payment solutions from Ripple can bring revolution broadly to the following scenarios:

- Real-time gross settlement
- Cross-border payment
- Micropayments
- Forex

However, that's not all.

Note: As per a Finextra news report back in 2016, people across the world send more than $155 trillion across borders, and this number is on an exponential rise year after year.

Ripple's first goal was to capture the international remittance market, which their small team is entirely engrossed in. However, that does not mean Ripple cannot be used elsewhere. The use cases that we will discuss later in this chapter can be reviewed by business leaders to realize the true power of Ripple in transforming the finance market we know today.

In order to understand where Ripple can be used, we need to understand the different types of financial markets.

As shown in *Figure 2.11* below, financial markets can be broadly divided into following four types:

- **Capital market**: Market where maturity of trading is for more than one year
- **Money market**: Market where maturity of trading is for less than one year
- **Equity market**: Stock market and quick trading
- **Forex market**: Market where trading can be done with different fiat currencies

Financial Markets

Capital Market

Money Market

FOREX Market

Equity Market

Figure 2.11: Types of financial markets

We will discuss some of these markets and find out how Ripple can dramatically improve ease of doing business in all these use cases in later chapters.

SWIFT versus Ripple

While comparing the features of SWIFT gpi and Ripple, one must consider all the pros and cons of both the networks before selecting one over other for their business need. *Figure 2.12* below can help greatly in such cases.

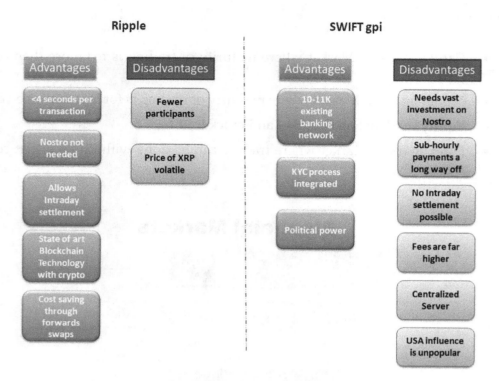

Figure 2.12: Ripple versus SWIFT gpi

Ripple and R3 Corda: The golden alliance

Until now we have discussed a lot on the inefficiencies in international remittance and how Ripple has the power to solve those issues. Although it's pretty much possible to use your existing traditional system to integrate with Ripple APIs (we will cover the development part in the next chapter), it's desirable to know how Ripple works in a distributed environment using a distributed ledger technology such as Blockchain. For doing so, let's discuss the sustainable combined architectural model of R3 Corda and Ripple that has been used in two very successful projects in the banking industry of Switzerland.

R3 Corda is one of the leading Blockchain-inspired private-permissioned distributed ledger technologies in the industry today. It's the Blockchain platform of choice for banks, FinTechs, and InsureTechs all across the globe for its high security, privacy, and fine-grained control of sharing data in a distributed environment. Let's discuss some of the basic features of Corda now.

Distributed ledger

Figure 2.13 below is the representation of a distributed ledger or Blockchain platform in general, where each node can be represented by an individual or an organization connected over a private or public network. The oracle node is an independent node that cannot be connected from outside the network but only through nodes within the network. It works in a neutral way for running services and calling external web services on behalf of any of the other nodes.

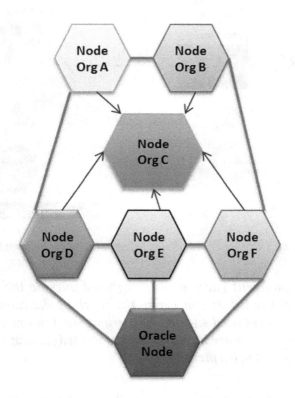

Figure 2.13 Distributed ledger

In most distributed ledger technologies or Blockchain-based systems, we usually keep data in a combination of on-chain (inside the Blockchain or DLT ledger) and off-chain (traditional RDBMS or IPFS ledger outside the main DLT ledger) databases. All user-related data goes to the off-chain database whereas transactional data, which needs to be shared between parties or nodes, is shared on the distributed or on-chain database.

Note that in *Figure 2.14* all nodes are shown to be connected by a single website with a shared off-chain database. But if needed, you can create a model where each of these nodes can have their individual off-chain ledger; it's up to your business requirement.

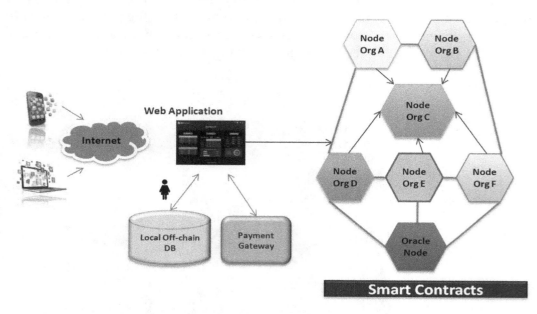

Figure 2.14: Solution architecture of distributed ledger with oracle node and off-chain database.

Note that here the payment gateway is integrated outside the ledger, and hence there is no way that the ledger can verify the work of the funding part directly. What if there is a business need such as delivery against payment where both legs (i.e., delivery and payment) are handled within the ledger hand in hand? What if there is a need of instant settlement?

Let's find out how Corda can help us in such a situation with a super-fast and scalable model providing adequate privacy.

R3 Corda features

While there are so many Blockchain protocols already available in market, what makes Corda unique? Well, here is a list.

• Unlike many others, Corda has been 100% **General Data Protection Regulation (GDPR)** compliant since its first release, which makes it business friendly to work in EU and most parts of the world.

- Corda has no dependency on a crypto currency. Wow!

- Smart contracts are written in Java and Kotlin, which are industry-standard languages.

- There is no sharing of data with unrelated nodes.

- Corda uses a different consensus mechanism from others where only the concerned parties in a transaction and a notary take the final decision of validating a transaction.

- Notary in Corda is not centralized but could be many maintained in a pool, and hence there is no single point of failure.

- Transactions are evaluated and confirmed only by the parties involved in the transaction rather than a broader pool of unrelated validators.

- Corda choreographs workflow between firms without a central controller.

- Corda is specialized for finance industry (but can work for all others).

In December 2018, R3 Corda partnered with Ripple and came up with a product called *Corda Settler*, where XRP Ledger can be invoked from Corda's neutral oracle node. *Figure 2.15* shows the solution architecture of a perfect distributed ledger, i.e., R3 Corda integrated with the XRP Ledger network through the neutral oracle node. In such a model, we can execute both delivery and payment legs of an international trade (domestic is also applicable) almost simultaneously, which would bring privacy, transparency, and peace of mind to both parties.

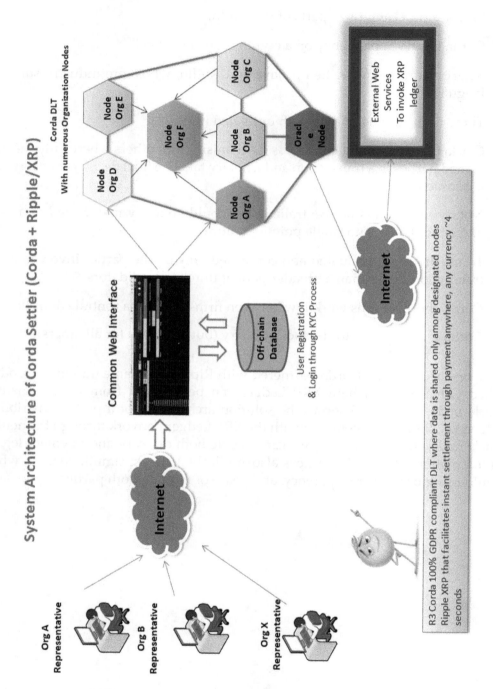

Figure 2.15: Architecture of R3 Corda Settler (Corda + Ripple/XRP)

Note that R3 Corda is a distributed ledger technology mainly focused on catering to B2B clients. In the above figure, all the nodes represent an independent organization and each of these organizations can have thousands of employees. In this model, we can create a single decentralized application where users of different organizations can register and provide their organization details and node addresses. Whenever there is a transaction request from a particular user, it would first hit the node it belongs to, and then would be shared with other related nodes. This data, once added, will remain there forever. If a user wishes to update this data, a new data will be created, yet the previous version will still stay there as historical data. The oracle node can connect to the web service you wish to get connected to. In Corda Settler, you can use this node to retrieve information such as the forex rate of XRP against any of the fiat currencies and can carry out instant payment using the XRP network.

Summary

In this chapter, we covered the following topics:

- How funds transfer works within the same bank, different banks within a country, and different bank across countries

- SWIFT network for international remittance and its pain points

- Architecture of XRP Ledger

- XRP and issued currencies

- Ripple products: xVia, xCurrent, and xRapid

- Ripple and R3 Corda: perfect Blockchain-based architecture

Questions

1. How much time does the SWIFT network take to transfer funds globally?

   A. One to five days

   B. Less than a minute

   C. Fraction of a second

2. What is SWIFT's advantage over Ripple?

   A. SWIFT is faster.

   B. SWIFT is cheaper.

   C. SWIFT is transparent.

   D. SWIFT has a strong network of ten to eleven thousand banks and has been operational for the past four to five decades.

3. What benefits can a bank achieve from Ripple adoption?

   A. International funds transfer would be faster, cheaper, and completely transparent.

   B. It is a highly scalable solution.

   C. There is no need of storing huge amounts of money in nostro and vostro accounts.

   D. All of the above.

4. What is the consensus model of Ripple's XRP Ledger?

   A. Completely centralized, i.e., one node decides validity of data before adding to ledger

   B. Completely decentralized, i.e., all nodes decide validity of data before adding to ledger

   C. Partially decentralized, i.e., a group of nodes decides validity of data before adding to ledger

5. What are the different use cases where Ripple can be used?

   A. Real-time gross settlement

   B. Cross-border payment

   C. Forex

   D. All of the above

6. Which one of these is an enterprise solution from Ripple?

A. xVia

B. xCurrent

C. xRapid

7. Which of the following products works only on XRP?

A. xVia

B. xCurrent

C. xRapid

8. Using xRapid we can exchange

A. Fiat to fiat

B. Crypto to crypto

C. Fiat to crypto and vice versa

D. All of the above

9. xCurrent is built on

A. XRP Ledger

B. Interledger

10. The four building blocks of xCurrent are as follows:

A. Messenger, Validator, ILP Ledger, and FX Ticker

B. Messenger, Validator, XRP Ledger, and FX Ticker

C. Messenger, Validator, Corda Ledger, and FX Ticker

D. AIDL, Validator, ILP Ledger, and FX Ticker

Answers

1 A, 2 D, 3 D, 4 C, 5 D, 6 B, 7 C, 8 D, 9 B, 10 A

References

- Liquidity Explained - https://ripple.com/insights/liquidity-explained/

- Ripple and XRP Can Cut Banks' Global Settlement Costs Up to 60 Percent - https://ripple.com/insights/ripple-and-xrp-can-cut-banks-global-settlement-costs-up-to-60-percent/

- SWIFT gpi Delivering the future of cross-border payments - https://www.swift.com/resource/swift-gpi-brochure

- SWIFT GPI vs Ripple Payments - https://www.finextra.com/blogposting/16147/swift-gpi-vs-ripple-payments

- Swift gpi crosses 50% threshold - https://www.finextra.com/pressarticle/76779/swift-gpi-crosses-50-threshold

- SWIFT & SEPA: How international money transfers actually work - https://blog.revolut.com/swift-sepa-how-international-money-transfers-actually-work/

- https://www.coindesk.com/xrp-fits-ripples-payments-products-explained

- https://www.binance.vision/economics/what-is-ripple

CHAPTER 3

Development with RippleNet and XRP

In this chapter, we will discuss the open source product of Ripple, known as XRP Ledger, using which banks and financial organizations can replace their age-old payment mechanisms with the payment mechanism of new generation that would bring a fast, low-cost, frictionless experience to their end clients.

Integrating XRP Ledger with any platform is simple, as the ledger has REST end-points for all its functions. It also has a Testnet network (https://s.altnet.rippletest.net:51234) that we can use for our development.

Create XRP account in Testnet

First, we have to create an XRP account on the Testnet faucet. As shown in *Figure 3.1*, visit the web page https://developers.ripple.com/xrp-test-net-faucet.html and click on the **Generate Credentials** button.

Home > Dev Tools > XRP Test Net Faucet

XRP Test Net Faucet

Ripple has created this alternative XRP Ledger test network with nodes in every region of the world to provide a testing platform for any software products built on the XRP Ledger without using real funds.

Test Net funds are intended for **testing** only. The Test Net ledger and balances will be reset on a regular basis.

> Generate credentials

Your Credentials

Address

rNuyi63N7MCkT7L9rTNWjUhnWfFVWw1DbL

Secret

sa9JDqPc6oFQm3oF3xJ5dgUoAEFPw

Balance

10,000 XRP

Figure 3.1: Creation of XRP account on ledger

As shown in the preceding screenshot, this newly created XRP account comes with an XRP address (i.e., **rNuyi63N7MCkT7L9rTNWjUhnWfFVWw1DbL**) and a secret key (i.e., **sa9JDqPc6oFQm3oF3xJ5dgUoAEFPw**). The account address is like a public key that can be shared with everyone, and the secret key, which is like a private key, should be shared only with the owner and should not be shared over the network. If the secret key is lost, then the user can no longer access the XRP account. At the same time, if the secret key falls in the wrong hands, then he/she can hack the account and transfer all the currencies to other accounts.

The XRP account created by Testnet comes with 10000 XRP by default. However, this is only a test network, and the amount in this account may get reset from time to time without prior warning. You can create as many accounts as you need for development and testing purposes.

Important factors of XRP account

Some of the important factors to remember while creating and maintaining an XRP account (both in test and production environments) are as follows.

- The account address is an alpha-numeric string of 25–35 characters that always starts with the letter *r*. This address never contains the number *0*, capital letter *O*, capital letter *I*, and lowercase letter *l*.

- The address is case sensitive.

- The important information in any account is the balance, history of transactions, and sequence number.

- Sequence number signifies how many times the XRP account has been deducted with XRPs. The correct sequence number is needed while requesting a new transaction.

- In order to keep the XRP account operational, one has to maintain a minimum reserve of 20 XRP in the account. Going below this minimum reserve would disqualify the account to transfer XRPs to other accounts. However, it will continue to exist on the XRP network, can receive XRPs from others, and transactions can be resumed on it by pumping it with minimum reserve.

- Once created, the XRP account stays there forever, even if it stays unused or inoperational.

Running a local rippled validating server

Here we are going to discuss some of the features of XRP Ledger exposed through its endpoint APIs. Most of the APIs on XRP Ledger follow the following pattern:

- Creation of an unsigned transaction offline
- Signing it with owner's secret key
- Submitting to XRP Ledger network

As the name suggests, the secret key (similar to a password) should be kept secret by the owner and should never be shared over a public network. Anyone who has access to the secret key can pass on the entire amount available in that account to elsewhere in no time. As XRP Ledger is based on Blockchain protocol, any transaction once complete cannot be reverted, and hence the XRPs would be entirely lost to hackers. Therefore, if your organization needs to do several transactions involving high value, it's advisable to run your own stand-alone or validating server. As shown in the following figure, signing part can be done on the local server with the secret key and then submitted to the global network for further processing.

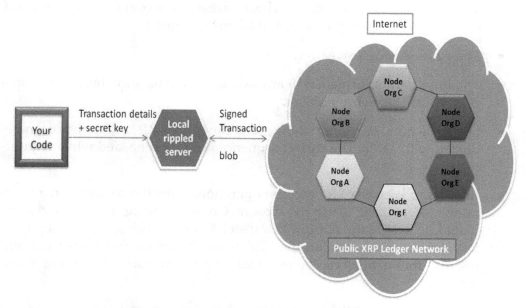

Figure 3.2: Running a local rippled server

The validating server can also connect to a network of other nodes, relay cryptographically signed transactions, and maintain a local copy of the complete shared global ledger. If you wish to run your own rippled server, you can follow the instructions on XRP Ledger's web page: https://xrpl.org/manage-the-rippled-server. html. The other option would be to code the signing part manually, which we will discuss now.

XRP Ledger endpoints

The XRP Ledger network comes with many different endpoints. Let's discuss some that are most widely used in related applications.

Retrieve account information (account_info)

Using **account_info**, endpoint information related to any XRP account can be retrieved from XRP Ledger. This retrieve function can be invoked by anyone who knows the address of the XRP account. However, this data is retrieved in read-only mode. For any transaction, or wherever there is a need of payment or transfer of money from the account, the secret key of the owner of the XRP account would be needed to sign the transaction. In this retrieve function, however, there is no need of the secret key. XRP Ledger is open to all for all its accounts information.

Listing 3.1 below is a JSON request of type POST for retrieving account information from Testnet (https://s.altnet.rippletest.net:51234), where **rNuyi63N7MCk-T7L9rTNWjUhnWfFVWw1DbL** is the XRP account address that we just created on Testnet.

```
{
   "method": "account_info",
   "params": [
      {
         "account": "rNuyi63N7MCkT7L9rTNWjUhnWfFVWw1DbL",
         "strict": true,
         "ledger_index": "current",
         "queue": true
      }
   ]
}
```

Listing 3.1: JSON request to retrieve account details

You can use any REST like POSTMAN or Chrome ARC to try this. Here, we have used Chrome ARC. *Listing 3.2* shows the response from the Testnet with all the details of a valid XRP account.

```
{
  "result": {
    "account_data": {
      "Account": "rNuyi63N7MCkT7L9rTNWjUhnWfFVWw1DbL",
      "Balance": "10000000000",
      "Flags": 0,
      "LedgerEntryType": "AccountRoot",
      "OwnerCount": 0,
      "PreviousTxnID": "744FA2D2FF81129107F1879BA595DD99-
F67D3197796EA92F41376853D1533FD2",
      "PreviousTxnLgrSeq": 19966064,
      "Sequence": 1,
      "index": "814B50DA4E691112D9D8BE702133D3B89AB6A5AB7172E9784586058-
A84E99FBB"
    },
    "ledger_current_index": 19966372,
    "queue_data": {
      "txn_count": 0
    },
    "status": "success",
    "validated": false
  }
}
```

Listing 3.2: JSON response with account details

Here, the most important data are the balance, which is 10000000000 XRP, and sequence number, which is 1. In *Figure 3.3* below, Chrome ARC has been used for sending a JSON request to the test network.

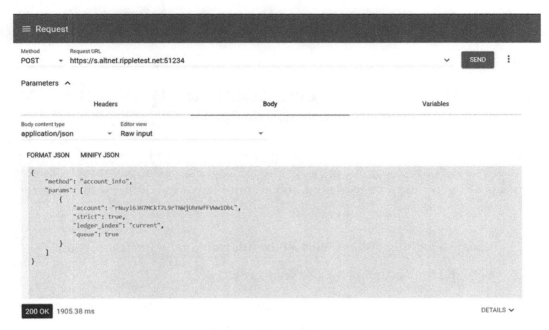

Figure 3.3: JSON request sent using Chrome ARC

Figure 3.4 shows the JSON response from the test network on Chrome ARC. As no XRP has been deducted from this account yet, hence **Sequence** is still 1, and the amount in **Balance** field is 10000000000. The request and response in text format are provided in *Listing 3.1* and *Listing 3.2*, respectively, for your reference and better visibility.

Figure 3.4: JSON response from test network on Chrome ARC

Each time an XRP is deducted from the account, the sequence number will increase by one. Let's discuss this in the next section.

Transfer XRPs between accounts (payment and submit)

For transferring XRPs through XRP Ledger, **submit** method needs to be invoked on the Testnet (https://s.altnet.rippletest.net:51234). However, payment of money through XRPs from source to destination account requires a little more effort. Following are the steps:

1. Create a payment object with all the information on the transaction.

2. Sign the transaction using the secret key.

3. Submit the transaction to XRP Ledger.

In fact, most of the transactions on XRP Ledger follow this pattern.

First, using Java (version 8), let's create a payment object and then sign it. You can do this using any standard language.

For example, create two different XRP accounts, **rsxHV15LNaczgzi3Br3KM7-c8FxNJzNRdZz** and **rnxFK8k6aBD1jZeLm481qAHzHMqCNWyphe**, on Testnet (https://s.altnet.rippletest.net:51234). You want to transfer 10000 XRP from **rsx-HV15LNaczgzi3Br3KM7c8FxNJzNRdZz** to **rnxFK8k6aBD1jZeLm481qAHzH-MqCNWyphe**. Create a **Payment** object by Ripple API and populate it with the following information:

1. Source XRP account

2. Destination XRP account

3. Amount to be transferred

4. Fee in drops

5. Sequence number retrieved by invoking **account_info** endpoint on source account **rsxHV15LNaczgzi3Br3KM7c8FxNJzNRdZz**

Use the secret key of the source account to sign this payment; the secret key should never be passed on the internet, for security purpose. Also, note that the ripple library is downloaded from https://github.com/ripple-unmaintained/ripple-lib-java/ and this library is kept on the classpath so that all the coretypes definitions used in this class can be used in this code. The code shown in *Listing 3.3* shows how to create a blob offline using ripple API.

```
/**We have created 2 different XRP accounts rsxHV15LNaczgzi3Br3KM7c8Fx-
NJzNRdZz
 * and rnxFK8k6aBD1jZeLm481qAHzHMqCNWyphe on Testnet https://s.altnet.
rippletest.net:51234
 * Now we are trying to transfer some amount from rsxHV15LNaczgzi3Br3K-
M7c8FxNJzNRdZz
 * to rnxFK8k6aBD1jZeLm481qAHzHMqCNWyphe*/


package com.java.client;


import com.ripple.core.coretypes.AccountID;

import com.ripple.core.coretypes.Amount;

import com.ripple.core.coretypes.STObject;

import com.ripple.core.coretypes.uint.UInt32;

import com.ripple.core.types.known.tx.signed.SignedTransaction;

import com.ripple.core.types.known.tx.txns.Payment;


public class RippleDemo {


    public static void main(String[] args) {


    /**The below secret key is that of XRP account rsxHV15LNaczgzi3-
Br3KM7c8FxNJzNRdZz*/
        String secret = "snwDnx5PXubVRbZAFGcgHDUt1gJAP";
        Payment payment = new Payment();

        payment.as(AccountID.Account,      "rsxHV15LNaczgzi3Br3KM7c8FxN-
JzNRdZz");

        payment.as(AccountID.Destination, "rnxFK8k6aBD1jZeLm481qAHzHMqC-
```

```
NWyphe");
        /**We intend to transfer 10000 XRPs from rsxHV15LNaczgzi3Br3KM7-
c8FxNJzNRdZz

        * to rnxFK8k6aBD1jZeLm481qAHzHMqCNWyphe account*/
        payment.as(Amount.Amount,          "10000");
        /**The sequence below is the sequence that we have receive in
response of account_info call

        * on account rsxHV15LNaczgzi3Br3KM7c8FxNJzNRdZz*/
        payment.as(UInt32.Sequence,         14);
        /**The fee for this account transfer we have set is 10 XRP which
is the minimum*/
        payment.as(Amount.Fee,             "10");


        SignedTransaction signed = payment.sign(secret);


        String tx_json = payment.prettyJSON();
        String blob = signAgain(tx_json, secret, signed);
    }


    private static String signAgain(String tx_json,
                                    String secret,
                                    SignedTransaction signedAlready) {
        // fromJSON will give us a payment object but we must cast it
        Payment txn = (Payment) STObject.fromJSON(tx_json);
        SignedTransaction signedAgain = txn.sign(secret);
        String blob = signedAgain.tx_blob.toString();
        System.out.println("blob: " + blob);
        return blob;
    }
}
```

Listing 3.3: Java code for creation of blob

You might wonder why we are allocating "10" in the "Fee" field. Well, this value is not in XRP but drops, which is a much smaller fraction of XRP. Please go through this website https://xrpl.org/transaction-cost.html to know more on the payment structure of XRP Ledger.

As of July 2019, the minimum transaction cost required by the network for a standard transaction is 0.00001 XRP (10 drops) or ~0.000004 USD.

Now, when you run this application, it will give you a blob data in return. In this case the value will be as follows:

120000228000000024000000E614000000000000027106840000000000000000A7321031CE86498688795DE5802BBA88F8DBCB52B6EE363CD37DC63DF-8C039318F0325374473045022100B2D638E0985677B25B6C6929FECDC3F-6B37A0C8C016ED18698BE5954D5C7817202201AB0524BAFB25222EC-7D14A9DC164C6600B804B8BA0B900B38B98D95121504B681142064E-6B2AF44091635E9293B32246D799F2A97A08314366EE2943532995F-358989A16149D43BAF9865A6

You can view this in the screenshot shown in *Figure 3.5*:

```
ParsingDemo.java    PostExample.java    RippleDemo.java
15  public class RippleDemo {
16
17      public static void main(String[] args) {
18          /**The below secret key is that of XRP account rsxHV15LNaczgzi3Br3KM7c8FxNJzNRdZz*/
19          String secret = "snwDnx5PXubVRbZAFGcgHDUt1gJAP";
20          Payment payment = new Payment();
21          payment.as(AccountID.Account,      "rsxHV15LNaczgzi3Br3KM7c8FxNJzNRdZz");
22          payment.as(AccountID.Destination, "rnxFK8k6aBD1jZeLm481qAHzHMqCNwyphe");
23          /**We intend to transfer 10000 XRPs from rsxHV15LNaczgzi3Br3KM7c8FxNJzNRdZz to rnxFK8k6aBD1jZeLm481qAHzHMqCNwyphe accou
24          payment.as(Amount.Amount,      "10000");
25          /**The sequence below is the sequence that we have receive in response of account_info call
26           * on account rsxHV15LNaczgzi3Br3KM7c8FxNJzNRdZz*/
27          payment.as(UInt32.Sequence,      14);
28          /**The fee for this account transfer we have set is 10 XRP which is the minimum*/
29          payment.as(Amount.Fee,      "10");
30          SignedTransaction signed = payment.sign(secret);
31          String tx_json = payment.prettyJSON();
32          String blob = signAgain(tx_json, secret, signed);
33      }
34
35      private static String signAgain(String tx_json, String secret, SignedTransaction signedAlready) {
36          // fromJSON will give us a payment object but we must cast it
37          Payment txn = (Payment) STObject.fromJSON(tx_json);
38          SignedTransaction signedAgain = txn.sign(secret);
39          String blob = signedAgain.tx_blob.toString();
40          System.out.println("blob: " + blob);
41          return blob;
42      }
43  }
44
```

```
Console
<terminated> RippleDemo [Java Application] C:\Program Files\Java\jre1.8.0_201\bin\javaw.exe (Jun 6, 2019, 2:49:44 PM)
blob: 120000228000000024000000E614000000000000027106840000000000000000A7321031CE86498688795DE5802BBA88F8DBCB52B6EE363CD37DC63DF8C03931
```

Figure 3.5: Value of blob

Next, as shown in *Figure 3.6*, this blob will be used to invoke the submit endpoint for actual funds transfer on the public XRP ledger. The following figure shows a JSON request to Testnet with the blob data in request.

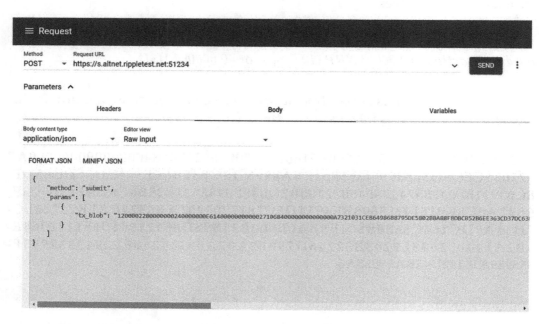

Figure 3.6: Blob sent to public XRP Ledger network for committing transaction

Figure 3.7 below shows a successful response from Testnet, again on Chrome ARC. It comes with status "**success**", **engine_result_code** 0, and **engine_result** "**tes-SUCCESS**".

Figure 3.7: Successful response

Listing 3.4 below shows the request in text format for developers who wish to try it on REST client on their own.

```
{
  "method": "submit",
  "params": [
    {
      "tx_blob": "1200002280000000240000000E614000000000000027106840000
0000000000A7321031CE86498688795DE5802BBA88F8DBCB52B6EE363CD37-
DC63DF8C039318F0325374473045022100B2D638E0985677B25B6C6929FECDC3F6-
B37A0C8C016ED18698BE5954D5C7817202201AB0524BAFB25222EC7D14A9DC164-
C6600B804B8BA0B900B38B98D95121504B681142064E6B2AF44091635E9293B32246D799-
F2A97A08314366EE2943532995F358989A16149D43BAF9865A6"
    }
  ]
}
```

Listing 3.4: Request in blob

Listing 3.5 shows the successful response from Testnet again with status "**success**", **engine_result_code** 0, and **engine_result "tesSUCCESS"**.

```
{
  "result": {
```

"engine_result": "tesSUCCESS",

"engine_result_code": 0,

"engine_result_message": "The transaction was applied. Only final in a validated ledger.",

"status": "success",

"tx_blob": "12000022800000002400000000E6140000000000002710684000000000 00000A7321031CE86498688795DE5802BBA88F8DBCB52B6EE363CD37DC63D-F8C039318F03253744730450221 00B2D638E0985677B25B6C6929FECDC3F6B37A0C8-C016ED18698BE5954D5C7817202201AB0524BAFB25222EC7D14A9DC164C6600B804B8-BA0B900B38B98D95121504B681142064E6B2AF44091635E9293B32246D799-F2A97A08314366EE2943532995F358989A16149D43BAF9865A6",

"tx_json": {

"Account": "rsxHV15LNaczgzi3Br3KM7c8FxNJzNRdZz",

"Amount": "10000",

"Destination": "rnxFK8k6aBD1jZeLm481qAHzHMqCNWyphe",

"Fee": "10",

"Flags": 2147483648,

"Sequence": 14,

"SigningPubKey": "031CE86498688795DE5802BBA88F8DBCB52B6EE363CD37-DC63DF8C039318F03253",

"TransactionType": "Payment",

"TxnSignature": "3045022100B2D638E0985677B25B6C6929FECDC3F6B37A0C8-C016ED18698BE5954D5C7817202201AB0524BAFB25222EC7D14A9DC164C6600B804B8-BA0B900B38B98D95121504B6",

"hash": "2B211E4845E40A71C813365911080F8EB62B6FD7149F7AFB10D58B61BA61-BE67"

}

}

}

Listing 3.5: Response showing success

Now both the sender and receiver can hit the **account_info** endpoint again for each of these two accounts to check whether the amount is really deducted and added to the destination account as expected. Also, the value of the sequence number must be one number higher than its previous value on the ledger just before this endpoint was invoked.

The other option you have is to run a local rippled server on premises, as specified in the previous section of this chapter, and send the payment details in a JSON request. A sample is shown in *Listing 3.6* with a secret key, although the amount is in fiat or issued currency.

```
{
  "method": "sign",
  "params": [
   {
     "offline": false,
     "secret": "snwDnx5PXubVRbZAFGcgHDUt1gJAP",
     "tx_json": {
       "Account": "rf1BiGeXwwQoi8Z2ueFYTEXSwuJYfV2Jpn",
       "Amount": {
         "currency": "USD",
         "issuer": "rf1BiGeXwwQoi8Z2ueFYTEXSwuJYfV2Jpn",
         "value": "1"
       },
       "Destination": "ra5nK24KXen9AHvsdFTKHSANinZseWnPcX",
       "TransactionType": "Payment"
     },
     "fee_mult_max": 1000
   }
  ]
}
```

Listing 3.6: Signing request to local rippled server

The response will be in the format shown in *Listing 3.7* and will come with a blob data.

```
{
  "result": {
    "status": "success",
    "tx_blob": "120000228000000024000001686 1D4838D7EA4C680000000000000000
0000000000000055534400000000004B4E9C06F24296074F7BC48F92A97916C6D-
C5EA9684000000000000002710732103AB40A0490F9B7ED8DF29D246BF2-
D6269820A0EE7742ACDD457BEA7C7D0931EDB7446304402200E5C2DD81FDF0-
BE9AB2A8D797885ED49E804DBF28E806604D878756410CA98B102203349581946B0D-
DA06B36B35DBC20EDA27552C1F167BCF5C6ECFF49C6A46F858081144-
B4E9C06F24296074F7BC48F92A97916C6DC5EA983143E9D4A2B8AA0780F682D136-
F7A56D6724EF53754",
    "tx_json": {
      "Account": "rf1BiGeXwwQoi8Z2ueFYTEXSwuJYfV2Jpn",
      "Amount": {
        "currency": "USD",
        "issuer": "rf1BiGeXwwQoi8Z2ueFYTEXSwuJYfV2Jpn",
        "value": "1"
      },
      "Destination": "ra5nK24KXen9AHvsdFTKHSANinZseWnPcX",
      "Fee": "10000",
      "Flags": 2147483648,
      "Sequence": 360,
      "SigningPubKey": "03AB40A0490F9B7ED8DF29D246BF2D6269820A0EE7742ACD-
D457BEA7C7D0931EDB",
      "TransactionType": "Payment",
      "TxnSignature": "304402200E5C2DD81FDF0BE9AB2A8D797885ED49E804D-
BF28E806604D878756410CA98B102203349581946B0DDA06B36B35DBC20E-
DA27552C1F167BCF5C6ECFF49C6A46F8580",
      "hash": "4D5D90890F8D49519E4151938601EF3D0B30B16CD6A519D9C99102-
C9FA77F7E0"
    }
  }
}
```

Listing 3.7: Response from local rippled server with blob

The blob in the response should be sent to the public XRP Ledger in a submit function as discussed before to commit the transaction on the public server. You can find more information at https://xrpl.org/send-xrp.html and https://xrpl.org/submit.html.

Partial payment

In direct payment scenarios, we specify the exact amount to deliver, after charging all kinds of fees. Hence, the actual amount deducted from the sender's account will be more than the amount specified. But using the partial payment feature, the sender can make sure to deduct the amount specified in the **Amount** field as the maximum limit and deduct all fees from it so that the receiver receives the amount with deductions of all fees. This can be achieved by using a flag called **tfPartial-Payment**. Let's explore this feature in detail.

The payment transaction that we discussed before was in XRP, but we can do so in issued currencies as well. In that case, a JSON request representing a **Payment** object has to be sent to a local rippled server as shown in *Listing 3. 8*:

```
{
  "TransactionType" : "Payment",
  "Account" : "rf1BiGeXwwQoi8Z2ueFYTEXSwuJYfV2Jpn",
  "Destination" : "ra5nK24KXen9AHvsdFTKHSANinZseWnPcX",
  "Amount" : {
    "currency" : "USD",
    "value" : "1",
    "issuer" : "rf1BiGeXwwQoi8Z2ueFYTEXSwuJYfV2Jpn"
  },
  "Fee": "12",
  "Flags": 2147483648,
  "Sequence": 2
}
```

Listing 3.8: JSON request for partial payment sent to local rippled server

Now the blob data in response has to be sent to the public server as discussed before. Here you can find that Amount is a complex field with currency information and value (in decimal). Please note that both the sender with address against **Account** as well as the receiver with address against **Destination** operate on the same fiat currency, i.e., USD. Here we can use a field called **tfPartialPayment**, which when set allows a payment to succeed by reducing the amount received instead of increasing the amount sent.

tfPartialPayment set to off

If **tfPartialPayment** flag is not used or disabled, then the **Amount** field, which is a complex field, specifies the exact amount to deliver, whereas the **SendMax** field, which is an optional field within **Amount**, specifies the maximum amount and currency to send. In such a case, if the amount specified in the **Amount** field cannot be delivered owing to some reason (e.g., funds just equal to the amount but not enough to pay the fees, or combination of amount and fees exceeds the **SendMax** amount) then the transaction fails. Had the fee been zero, then such a transaction would have passed.

So, under any condition, the **SendMax** value should be added to the funds and the amount sent should be less than that.

Amount + (fees) = (sent amount) ≤ SendMax

tfPartialPayment set to on

If the **tfPartialPayment** flag is enabled, partial payments can work in spite of limitations such as fees, not enough liquidity, not enough space in the receiving account's trust lines, and so on.

In such a scenario, we often use two optional parameters, **DeliverMin** and **Send-Max**. The partial payment transaction is successful if it delivers any amount equal or greater than the amount specified in the **DeliverMin** field and less than or equal to the amount specified in the **SendMax** field.

With this flag we, can use the **delivered_amount** metadata field to define the intended partial payment; in other words, we can keep a big amount in the **Amount** field and a small amount in the **delivered_amount** field. In this case, the actual amount delivered to the receiver would be **delivered_amount**.

This feature can be risky if not used judiciously. Let's find out why.

Illegal Use Case

A malicious user sends in issued currency for a delivery against payment scenario where the **Amount** field has a large number. However, the **tfPartialPayment field** is enabled and the amount in **delivered_amount** metadata is too small. In such a case, if the payment goes through and the receiver verifies only the **Amount** field then he assumes it's a full payment and hands over the deliverables. The malicious user simply absconds with the product or services received from the seller before the seller realizes his mistake.

Legal Use Case

One may wonder why partial payment still exists as a feature in Ripple. Well it can be really helpful in certain scenarios. Consider the following example:

Let's say there is a buyer party for an e-Auction who registers himself to the auction house. The auction house needs some collateral for participation in the auction so that money would be deducted from that collateral if a suitable match is found. However, the auction ends and the buyer is unable to find any suitable product to buy or let's just say all the collateral money is not spent. In that case, the auction house has to return the amount to the buyer. However, why should the auction house bear the fees and transaction cost? Hence, the auction house exploits the partial payment feature to send the amount after deducting all the fees and related cost from the amount and without incurring additional costs to self. The buyer would have no issue in such case.

Note: Only issued currencies are eligible for partial payment, because in case of Amount in XRP, the transaction cost is always deducted from the sender's account, regardless of the type of transaction.

You can find more information at https://developers.ripple.com/partial-payments.html.

Cross-currency payments

In the previous chapter we have already discussed that using XRP Ledger we can transfer XRP as well as issued currencies or fiat currencies. However, using the cross-currency payments feature, we can transfer funds in both types of currencies as well as digital tokens that are only issued within XRP Ledger, with no outside backing.

A cross-currency payment involves at least two currencies; hence, it can be referred to as a **decentralized exchange** on XRP Ledger used to exchange different kinds of currencies. It's mandatory that at least one currency involved must be a non-XRP issued currency and the other may or may not be XRP. Also, with cross-currency payments we can deliver a fixed amount or do partial payment, as discussed above. Now how exactly does that work?

First a user must create an offer object as shown in *Listing 3.9*:

```
{
    "TransactionType": "OfferCreate",
    "Account": "ra5nK24KXen9AHvsdFTKHSANinZseWnPcX",
    "Fee": "12",
    "Flags": 0,
    "LastLedgerSequence": 7108682,
    "Sequence": 8,
    "TakerGets": "6000000",
    "TakerPays": {
      "currency": "GKO",
      "issuer": "ruazs5h1qEsqpke88pcqnaseXdm6od2xc",
      "value": "2"
    }
}
```

Listing 3.9: JSON request for partial payment sent to local rippled server

In such a case, the JSON request representing an **OfferCreate** object to be sent to a local rippled server will be as shown in the listing, whose blob data in response has to be sent to the public server as discussed before. The public ledger matches the order with others and can get this traded. Here, the trading could be a complete matching or partial matching. Also, an offer created can be cancelled and removed from the ledger through **OfferCancel** transaction type.

You can find more on cross-currency payments on this website: https://xrpl.org/cross-currency-payments.html.

Escrow payment

Escrow is the killer feature of Ripple's XRP Ledger using which a certain amount of XRPs can be locked in an escrow account of a payer to be paid to the payee later. The amount can be released after a predetermined end time is reached or a cryptographic condition has been fulfilled. After getting released, the situation is re-evaluated and the amount can be either delivered to the payee or cancelled so that it returns to the original account.

It's noteworthy that escrows work only with XRP and not with any other issued currencies.

Following is the entire process of escrow:

1. First calculate the **FinishAfter** parameter as shown in *Figure 3.8*. This value represents a future time in seconds when the funds will be released either to get paid to the destination account or be cancelled. Here we are specifying the time as a whole number in seconds since the Ripple Epoch, which is 946684800 seconds after the UNIX epoch. For example, to release funds at midnight UTC on July 25, 2019, you will have to deduct **946684800** from this future time in seconds. The result is **617373645**. Use this time for creating the escrow.

```
 1  package com.java.client;
 2
 3  import java.text.ParseException;
 4  import java.text.SimpleDateFormat;
 5  import java.util.Date;
 6
 7  public class RippleEscrowDemo {
 8
 9      public static void main(String[] args) throws ParseException {
10          String releaseDate = "2019/07/25 18:10:45";
11          SimpleDateFormat sdf = new SimpleDateFormat("yyyy/MM/dd HH:mm:ss");
12          Date date = sdf.parse(releaseDate);
13          long releaseTimeinSeconds = date.getTime() / 1000;
14          long release_date_ripple = releaseTimeinSeconds - 946684800;
15
16          System.out.println("releaseTimeinSeconds: " + releaseTimeinSeconds + " ripple time: " + release_date_ripple);
17      }
18  }
19
```

```
Console
<terminated> RippleEscrowDemo [Java Application] C:\Program Files\Java\jre1.8.0_201\bin\javaw.exe (Jun 21, 2019, 6:25:05 PM)
releaseTimeinSeconds: 1564058445 ripple time: 617373645
```

Figure 3.8: Calculation of FinishAfter parameter, i.e., release_data_ripple

2. Create Escrow object of source **Account** with **Amount** and **Destination Address** through **EscrowCreate** transaction. Note that the library downloaded from the ripple library (https://github.com/ripple-unmaintained/ripple-lib-java/) is already kept on classpath and is not updated for coretype **EscrowCreate;** you can do it on your own. Once it's defined, the code will be similar to *Listing 3.10* below, where the sender signs with the secret key to produce the blob.

```
package com.java.client;
```

```java
import java.text.ParseException;
import java.text.SimpleDateFormat;
import java.util.Date;

import com.ripple.core.coretypes.AccountID;
import com.ripple.core.coretypes.Amount;
import com.ripple.core.coretypes.STObject;
import com.ripple.core.coretypes.uint.UInt32;
import com.ripple.core.types.known.tx.signed.SignedTransaction;
import com.ripple.core.types.known.tx.txns.Payment;
import com.ripple.core.types.known.tx.txns.EscrowCreate;

public class RippleEscrowDemo {

    public static void main(String[] args) throws ParseException {

        String secret = "snwDnx5PXubVRbZAFGcgHDUt1gJAP";

        String releaseDate = "2019/07/25 18:10:45";

        SimpleDateFormat sdf = new SimpleDateFormat("yyyy/MM/dd
HH:mm:ss");

        Date date = sdf.parse(releaseDate);

        long releaseTimeinSeconds = date.getTime() / 1000;

        long release_date_ripple = releaseTimeinSeconds - 946684800;


        System.out.println("releaseTimeinSeconds: " + releaseTimeinSec-
onds + " ripple time: " + release_date_ripple);

        EscrowCreate escrowCreate = new EscrowCreate();

        escrowCreate.as(AccountID.Account,       "rsxHV15LNaczgzi3Br3KM7-
c8FxNJzNRdZz");
```

```
    escrowCreate.as(AccountID.Destination, "rnxFK8k6aBD1jZeLm481qAH-
zHMqCNWyphe");

    escrowCreate.as(Amount.Amount,          "10000");

    escrowCreate.as(FinishAfter,            617373645);

      SignedTransaction signed = escrowCreate.sign(secret);
      String tx_json = escrowCreate.prettyJSON();
      String blob = signAgain(tx_json, secret, signed);
      System.out.println("blob: " + blob);

  }


    private static String signAgain(String tx_json, String secret,
SignedTransaction signedAlready) {
      // fromJSON will give us a payment object but we must cast it

    EscrowCreate txn = (EscrowCreate) STObject.fromJSON(tx_json);
      SignedTransaction signedAgain = txn.sign(secret);
      String blob = signedAgain.tx_blob.toString();
      System.out.println("blob: " + blob);
      return blob;

  }
}
```

Listing 3.10: Creation of blob against EscrowCreate object

3. Now you can submit the blob to Testnet (or real server if in production) just like you did in the direct payment transaction.

4. Wait for the **FinishAfter** time to be over.

5. As shown in *Listing 3.11*, **EscrowFinish** transaction can be created if business condition is fulfilled. For this, again follow a similar pattern as **EscrowCreate**. Create a JSON object, sign it, and submit the blob to the server. Here as well, you have to do some work on Ripple's library for Java, as these types and coretypes are undefined in the library.

```java
package com.java.client;

import java.text.ParseException;
import java.text.SimpleDateFormat;
import java.util.Date;

import com.ripple.core.coretypes.AccountID;
import com.ripple.core.coretypes.Amount;
import com.ripple.core.coretypes.STObject;
import com.ripple.core.coretypes.uint.UInt32;
import com.ripple.core.types.known.tx.signed.SignedTransaction;
import com.ripple.core.types.known.tx.txns.Payment;
import com.ripple.core.types.known.tx.txns.EscrowFinish;

public class RippleEscrowFinishDemo {

    public static void main(String[] args) throws ParseException {

        String secret = "snwDnx5PXubVRbZAFGcgHDUt1gJAP";

        String releaseDate = "2019/07/25 18:10:45";

        SimpleDateFormat sdf = new SimpleDateFormat("yyyy/MM/dd HH:mm:ss");

        Date date = sdf.parse(releaseDate);

        long releaseTimeinSeconds = date.getTime() / 1000;

        long release_date_ripple = releaseTimeinSeconds - 946684800;
        System.out.println("releaseTimeinSeconds: " + releaseTimeinSec-
onds + " ripple time: " + release_date_ripple);

        EscrowFinish escrowFinish = new EscrowFinish();
```

```
    escrowFinish.as(AccountID.Account,      "rsxHV15LNaczgzi3Br3KM7-
c8FxNJzNRdZz");

    escrowFinish.as(Owner,        "rsxHV15LNaczgzi3Br3KM7c8FxN-
JzNRdZz");

    escrowFinish.as(OfferSequence,        1);

  SignedTransaction signed = escrowFinish.sign(secret);
  String tx_json = escrowFinish.prettyJSON();
  String blob = signAgain(tx_json, secret, signed);
  System.out.println("blob: " + blob);
 }


    private static String signAgain(String tx_json, String secret,
SignedTransaction signedAlready) {
   // fromJSON will give us a payment object but we must cast it

  EscrowFinish txn = (EscrowFinish) STObject.fromJSON(tx_json);
  SignedTransaction signedAgain = txn.sign(secret);
  String blob = signedAgain.tx_blob.toString();
  System.out.println("blob: " + blob);
  return blob;
 }
}
```

Listing 3.11: Creation of blob against EscrowFinish object

Submit the blob to the server as you did in the direct payment JSON request to release the amount to destination.

6. Anyone can submit **EscrowCancel** transaction if the escrow has expired.

For this, you have to work on the library to create **EscrowCancel** and specify the **Account, Owner,** and **OfferSequence** coretypes. Here the **Account** field belongs to the account that is cancelling it, and it can be anyone. **Owner** is the escrow account, and **OfferSequence** is the sequence number received in response to **Es-**

crowCreate. The rest of the process of creation and submission of blob remains the same.

Note that this entire process is equivalent to a **Websocket** request, as shown in *Listing 3.12:*

```
{
  "id": 2,
  "command": "submit",
  "secret": "snwDnx5PXubVRbZAFGcgHDUt1gJAP",
  "tx_json": {
    "Account": "rsxHV15LNaczgzi3Br3KM7c8FxNJzNRdZz",
    "TransactionType": "EscrowCreate",
    "Amount": "10000",
    "Destination": "rnxFK8k6aBD1jZeLm481qAHzHMqCNWyphe",
    "FinishAfter": 617373645
  }
}
```

Listing 3.12: Creation of blob for EscrowCreate object through local rippled server

However, we are taking all these pains just to ensure the secret key is not exposed over the public internet, which could be risky. We can also use the local rippled server approach to keep development short and simple.

Holding the payment amount in a separate account from where transactions are forbidden until a predetermined time is reached or a condition is fulfilled can bring peace of mind for the payer as well as the payee. In Chapter 8, we will discuss how this feature can be used in a judicious manner to improve delivery against payment processes in trade finance and make trading transparent as well as risk free.

Note: Escrow works best for high-value, low-quantity payments. As funds transfer involves different scenarios such as creation, finish, or cancel, each involving fees, Escrows are more expensive than regular payments. If there is a need of fast, low-value payments, channels are a better solution.

You can learn more from https://developers.ripple.com/escrow.html and https://xrpl.org/use-escrows.html to know about all its libraries.

Checks

Checks are like paper check payments in real life, where there is a source account, destination account, specific maximum amount, and date of expiry. Also, both the parties can cancel the check at any time before the date of expiry. Unlike direct payment, a check does not create an obligation to the issuer for transferring the funds. The check can fail owing to lack of funds, and you can try to cash it again until its date of expiry. The actual transaction of money will occur at the time of the receiver cashing the check. Below, *Table 3.1* shows a list of parameters in a JSON request for creating the check.

Field	Data Type	Internal Type	Description
Destination	String	Account	Source account i.e. "rUn84CUYbN-jRoTQ6mSW7BVJPSVJNLb1QLo"
SendMax	Currency Amount	Amount	Maximum amount that can be deducted from source and deposited at destination
Expiration	Number	UInt32	Time in seconds since Ripple Epoch at which the check expires
InvoiceID	String	Hash256	
Fee	String	Fee	Transaction fee in drops

Table 3.1: Parameters for check request

The JSON request representing a **CheckCreate** object to be sent to a local rippled server would be as shown below, whose blob data in response has to be sent to the public server.

```
{
   "TransactionType": "CheckCreate",
   "Account": "rBXsgNkPcDN2runsvWmwxk3Lh97zdgo9za",
   "Destination": "rGPnRH1EBpHeTF2QG8DCAgM7z5pb75LAis",
   "SendMax": "100000000",
   "InvoiceID": "46060241FABCF692D4D934BA2A6C4427CD4279083E38C77-
   CBE642243E43BE291"
}
```

Listing 3.13: JSON request for CheckCreate object

Note that, using checks, we can send both XRPs as well as issued currencies to the receiver. The source account can be debited only with its type of currency and credit the destination. The above request is for currency XRP. In case of any other issued currencies, we have to specify the details of the amount, as shown in *Table 3.1*:

Field	Data Type	Internal Type	Description
Currency	String	Currency	Three-character currency codes, which you can find here https://www.xe.com/iso4217.php
Value	String	Amount	Amount in decimal, e.g.,100.55
Issuer	String	Account	Issuer account, e.g., rUn84CUYb-NjRoTQ6mSW7BVJPSVJNL-b1QLo

Table 3.1: Details of Amount object

So, the entire life cycle of a check goes as following:

- The issuer can create a check using **CheckCreate** transaction type, which can be signed by the issuer's secret key, and the blob is submitted to the network.

- After **CheckCreate**, a Check JSON object is created on XRP Ledger that lists all the information of Check as defined by the transaction that created it. Most importantly, it has **InvoiceID,** which is also **CheckID**, a 64-character hexadecimal string.

- The receiver, within the time of expiry, can cash an amount up to maximum limit using **CheckCash** transaction with **CheckID**.

- Either the source or the destination can remove the check from the ledger by using **CheckCancel** transaction type with **CheckID** within the expiration time of the check. If the check has expired, any account on the ledger can do so.

Checks can be executed and tested on the XRP Ledger test network. This facility is not yet enabled in production and is planned for a future release. You can learn more from https://developers.ripple.com/checks.html and https://xrpl.org/checks.html.

Payment channels

XRP Ledger comes with a very special feature called *payment channels* using which users can send and receive funds asynchronously over the network. This is especially useful where the sender needs to send a small amount of money multiple times to the receiver over a time period. In such a case, a separate channel is established against which payers can send XRPs multiple times until the channel expires. Finally, all the transactions are settled in bulk once and for all.

Let's consider a situation as shown in *Figure 3.9* below. Organization X needs cabs for its employees within the city and needs services of cab company Organization Y. They sign a contract for next one month, as per which every time a cab is summoned by Organization X, 10 XRP are to be paid from Organization X to Organization Y. So, they create a payment channel for the next one month for a maximum amount of 1000 XRP where Organization X is the sender and Organization Y is the receiver. After one month, the payment channel can be dissolved. Refer the figure below for the working cycle of a payment channel.

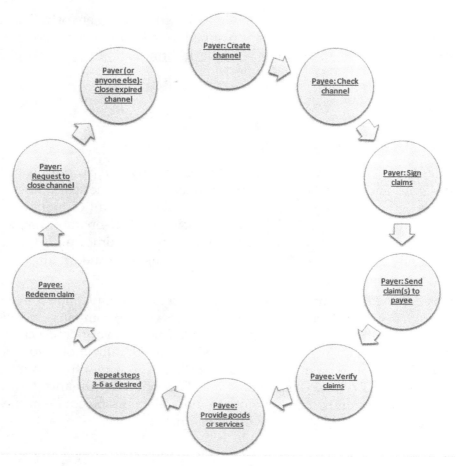

Figure 3.9: Life cycle of a payment channel

If you wish to run a payment channel, you have to configure your local rippled server first. The details of the configuration can be found on XRP Ledger's website: https://xrpl.org/use-payment-channels.html.

The asynchronous processing of transactions can be beneficial for specific business scenarios.

Where the throughput of Ripple transactions in general is claimed to be as high as 15000 TPS with payment channels, it can go much higher. The XRP Ledger website says, "Research has demonstrated the ability to create over Ed25519 100,000 signatures per second and to verify over 70,000 per second on commodity hardware in 2011."

Create XRP account in production

Similar to opening an account in a traditional bank, we need to open a real XRP account using a crypto wallet before going into production. In fact, to be fully operational, we need to open such accounts for each of the users participating in the application.

As per the features offered, the wallets can be divided into three types:

1. Mobile wallets

2. Software wallets

3. Hardware wallets

The users are free to choose any one of them as per their requirements and the safety features needed for their business. They can also keep the information on paper wallets; however, there is risk of losing it or it being stolen or misplaced.

Software wallet

A software wallet, also known as Toast Wallet, can be installed on your computer. Exodus is a very popular software wallet provider for XRP and is user-friendly and safe.

Mobile wallet

Unlike a software wallet, a mobile version, which is extremely popular among XRP traders, is installed on the user's mobile device. Such wallets are free of charge and can be downloaded from smartphones.

Hardware wallet

Hardware wallets are considered the safest as they encrypt the data and keep it safe in offline mode. Ledger Nano S wallets are popular in this space.

How does one send XRPs?

If you would like to send XRPs to someone, you copy the recipient's wallet address and enter it at the **Send** tab in your wallet. You then just enter the amount of XRP you would like to send out and complete the transaction.

Something to keep in mind is the minimum XRP balance you need to have for your address to be considered valid by the network. The ripple protocol has implemented a *rule* that no other crypto currency has. Everyone needs to have a minimum balance in their wallet before they can send out any coins. Currently the minimum balance is 20 XRP. This number can be changed by Ripple if, for example, the price suddenly rises or falls by a large margin.

Example: If the total balance of your ripple wallet is 50 XRP, you are able to send out a maximum of 30 XRP. The remaining 20 XRP need to stay in your wallet and can't be sent out owing to the requirements of the protocol.

How does one buy XRPs?

Buying real XRPs would be the last nail before moving on to production. You can buy as many XRPs you want through the following two processes:

- You can buy using your credit or debit card. It works best with USD with exchanges such as Bitstamp.

- You can purchase them from any of the crypto exchanges such as Coinbase or Binance, as shown in *Figure 3.10*, where you can also check the current exchange rate before buying. Through this process you can even exchange your existing bitcoins, Ethers, or any other sellable crypto currencies with XRPs.

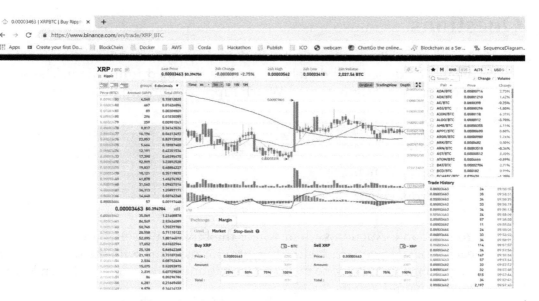

Figure 3.10: Purchasing and exchanging crypto currencies on Binance crypto exchange

The good news is that, in case you do not wish to work with XRPs any more, you can always sell them and stick to any fiat currencies you consider safe. But why would you?

Summary

In this chapter, we covered the following topics:

- Creation of free XRP account on XRP Ledger's test network

- Running a local rippled server

- Features of XRP Ledger such as direct payment, partial payment, check, escrow, payment channels, and cross-currency payments and how to use them in applications

- Purchasing XRPs and storing them in different types of wallets

Questions

1. You wish to have an international trading system where the payment should be done immediately on a predetermined future date. The seller needs assurance of payment. Which Ripple feature would you use?

   A. Check

   B. Escrow

   C. Direct payment

   D. Micropayment

2. You got an e-Auction system where the buyer and seller are unknown to each other. However, after the buy order is matched with the sell order, settlement needs to be done instantly with immediate payment. Which Ripple feature would you use?

   A. Check

   B. Escrow

   C. Direct payment

   D. Micropayment

3. Who can cancel a check before the date of expiry?

   A. The issuer

   B. The receiver

   C. Any of the above two

   D. Any account holder on the ledger

4. Can you freeze an issued currency on an account on a ledger?

   A. Yes

   B. No

5. Can you freeze XRP on an account on a ledger?

   A. Yes

   B. No

6. What is the significance of sequence number in the account?

   A. It tells us how many deductions have been done on the account and is used in payment requests.

   B. It tells the version number of the ledger.

   C. It tells us how many transactions are possible on the account.

   D. It tells the number of failed attempts.

Answers

1 B, 2 C, 3 C, 4 A, 5 B, 6 A

CHAPTER 4

Use Case: Micropayments

In the previous chapter, we discussed payment channels and how asynchronous payment can create many new business models in international trading. In this chapter, we will discuss the feature further with micropayment use cases.

Note that the term *micropayment* often refers to a payment of a very small amount of money, usually under $10 to $12 and could be as low as $0.0001. Hence, you can refer to this model for any other micro-funding project that you are involved in, especially in the international market.

Business scenario: Amazon and PayPal

Now consider a scenario where a retail customer from India found a fancy item on Amazon, USA,(https://www.amazon.com/) that is unavailable on Amazon India (https://www.amazon.in/). However, her credit card is not accepted on Amazon USA, or let's say her payment is simply rejected because the billing address is outside the USA. In such cases, you need an alternate payment mechanism that would work on a global basis. Today, many business models work on micropayments.

One of the most widely used global platforms used under such circumstances is PayPal, which has a platform for micropayments. PayPal considers any payment under $12 as a micropayment. [1] As of now, one needs to have a business or premier account with PayPal for executing such micropayments. Hence, the user has to pay extra to create and maintain such an account. In addition, as specified on the PayPal website, it charges quite high fees for all payments be it micro or otherwise.

Challenges in micropayments

Some of the challenges incurred by the industry related to micropayments are as follows:

- A global network is required with no single point of failure so that business can run uninterrupted 365 days a year, 7 days a week, and 24 hours a day.

- Security of the network is paramount.

- The system should operate on any recognized currency, even loyalty points.

- Advanced features like escrow, cancellation, or expiration of payment should exist, based on some validation logic or smart contract.

- Fees should be minimum.

Examples

Some of the examples of micropayments are listed below, but the list could go much longer.

IoT messaging

Internet of Things (IoT) is a futuristic technology where sensor-based devices can communicate with each other through the internet. Let's say you are driving your car and looking out for a parking space in nearby parking lots. In such a scenario, you can get connected to the parking network that would be able to tell you the exact coordinates of the parking spaces, their prices, and other details, which would make your life easier. Such information would be available on a pay-as-you-go basis and would need micropayments, sometimes even in cents.

Charity

Many charitable organizations ask for donations and you may feel like spending a couple of bucks, which might be worth a significant amount in certain countries in Asia, Africa, or South America. However, most payment mechanisms do not allow you to donate below a particular amount, and hence your hands are tied. In such a scenario, XRP can work as a godsend.

Services

There are many pay-as-you-go services that you use on a day-to-day basis. For example, software services, the games that you play on your android devices or iPhone, or even ISD calls work on this model for a very small amount of payment.

Microfinance

Microfinance deals with investments of small amounts, especially for people who do not have access to regular banking and financial institutions for financial transactions. It largely falls into two categories: microlending and microinsurance.

Microinsurance is usually applied for securing livelihood for people falling under the low-income group earning below $4 a day. For example, farmers can be insured for loss of crops against bad weather or accidental loss so that their families are safeguarded with minimal earning per annum.

Microlending, also known as micro-credit, on the other hand involves granting small amount of loans to borrowers who are mostly from unprivileged class lacking collateral or a verifiable credit history.

Solution with Ripple/XRP

As stated in Chapter 3, XRP Ledger's payment channels feature is just suitable for retail market dealers where service providers and service consumers wish to establish a temporary, super-fast, and low-fee payment network with each other locally or globally. They need to create accounts on XRP Ledger and establish a payment channel with a specified time limit and amount. A cheap, fast, risk-free, and efficient micropayment system like Ripple/XRP would give rise to many new business models in a future world, which exist only at a conceptual level as of now. You can convert any local currency to XRP and convert it back to another local currency by transforming your micro-funding platform to a global level using this feature.

XRP for micropayments in news

As per a news report in April 2019, "'XRP May Soon Get Integrated Into Skype', says Weiss Rating." As requested by Ripple lovers, Microsoft is considering this feature to boost their business. [2]

Rumours are doing the rounds that e-commerce giant eBay, with a business network spanning 190 countries, too may opt for Ripple/XRP for its payments. [3]

Summary

In this chapter, we covered the following topics:

- Working models of e-commerce sites and their business limitations due to inefficiencies in payments
- Challenges in micropayment model
- How Ripple can help

References

1. How can I update my payment preferences for micropayments? - https://www.paypal.com/gf/smarthelp/article/how-can-i-update-my-payment-preferences-for-micropayments-faq1691

2. XRP May Soon Get Integrated Into Skype, Says Weiss Rating - https://www.btcnn.com/cryptocurrency-news/xrp-may-soon-get-integrated-into-skype-says-weiss-rating/

3. Ripple (XRP) Stands A Better Chance If E-Bay Crypto Payment Rumour Comes to Reality. Here's Why - https://todaysgazette.com/ripple-xrp-stands-a-better-chance-if-e-bay-crypto-payment-rumour-comes-to-reality-heres-why/

CHAPTER 5

Use Case: Instant Security Settlement in Stock Market

Auction is a public platform where different parties openly come together, bid for their products and services, and sell them off to the highest bidder. With time, the auction process has evolved from a physical format to demat, as well as from local to online, to promote ease of doing business and cut down on human errors. Also, there have been many rounds of improvements in the matching logic in buy and sell orders as per market requirements. However, over the past so many years, one property of auction that has remained the same is that it's a classic example of (instant) delivery against payment.

In this chapter, we will discuss how the risks related to delivery against payment and settlement can be minimized by using Ripple's instant money transfer mechanism. This model can be used both in the national as well as international space, where trading was not possible before owing to currency regulation issues.

Business scenario

Let's explore the auction process and the various phases of Bombay Stock Exchange. [1] The buy or sell orders initiated by traders can be of three types:

- **Limit order**: Where the exact rate of the stock is mentioned by the investor. The limit orders have the risk of not getting traded or partially traded as the market movement might be different from expectation.

- **Market order**: Where rate is not mentioned and it varies with the current best market rate. Market orders will always find a match as there will always be buyers and sellers in the market. However, they might not be traded at the price wanted.

- **Stop order**: A special kind of order that has the benefit of both worlds. Just like market order, the stop order is traded with the best available rate, but only if a particular rate is reached. Hence, in case of a buy order, the price must be above the current price, and for a sell order, the stop price must be below the current price.

Most stock exchanges in the world follow a similar pattern. The schedule goes as follows.

Pre-open Session (9.00 a.m. – 9.15 a.m.): Traders can place buy and sell orders and can modify or cancel them during this time.

Continuous Session (9.15 a.m. – 3.30 p.m.): In this session, the exchange matches the orders as per price and time and trading is confirmed.

Closing Session (3.30 p.m. – 3.40 p.m.): No trading happens during this phase, and the closing price is calculated.

Post Closing Session (3.40 p.m. – 4.00 p.m.): At post closing the trading can happen only at the closing price.

T + 2 Settlement: The pay-in and pay-out of money and stocks (i.e., delivery against payment) happens after two days, which is called the settlement of trading. **[2]**

Now let's consider some of the pain points of the modern pattern of e-Auction.

Challenges in e-Auction

Consider a scenario where multiple business houses wish to come together and indulge in buying and selling of their shares. This system may involve organizations that wish to do an **initial product offering (IPO)** or parties who simply wish to buy and sell and earn money. Let's elaborate an electronic auction or e-Auction use case that has multiple pain points:

- **Fraud**: Most auctions in the world deal with delivery against payment. The biggest issue in such a system is synchronization between both legs at the same time.

- **Limited participation**: Settlement becomes a bigger issue if the business deal is between parties in an international arena, as there is involvement of multiple currencies.

- **Long settlement**: This is the most cumbersome part in an auction as, in most parts of the world, settlement takes T+1 or T+2 days owing to regulatory issues. Delay in payment jeopardizes business.

Instant settlement: The golden goose

One of the major advantages of instant settlement is that delivery against payment could be made much faster. Also, this real-time business model makes end client much more content as fraudulence is also under control. Customers today are willing to pay a fee for such services that can bring clarity to the business model. Demat accounts, which was a new model two decades back, have become a global standard today for share trading. Similarly, payment using crypto or digital currencies will be a default minimum for business houses, as business leaders will realize how much extra they are paying or the risk they are incurring with the same old outdated payment systems.

Solution

Ripple can provide solutions to most of these requirements. When it comes to minimizing fraud, currency issue, or settlement delay, there could be two different solutions to this business scenario.

- Tokenization model
- Ripple/XRP

Let's explore both.

Tokenization model

The first one uses a tokenization approach. Here, the buyers first buy tokens from the auction platform in exchange of fiat currency. Now their money is represented on the ledger as tokens even before the actual auction starts. All the buy and sell orders will be taken care of by those tokens already purchased, and trading as well as settlement will be immediate. At the end of the auction, the remaining tokens can be cashed back by the buyers.

However, the issue with this model is that if the buyer is in need of more money, then the entire conversion will take time and that might not be feasible for a limited-time auction. Perhaps we are in need of a more real-time solution where money can be pushed into the ecosystem as and when needed.

Ripple-based settlement

Let's refer to *Figure 5.1* below where R3 Corda is used as a Blockchain-inspired decentralized ledger technology, which works in close association with Ripple. Corda also has its open source solution for integration, called Corda Settler whose code is freely available on GitHub in Kotlin.

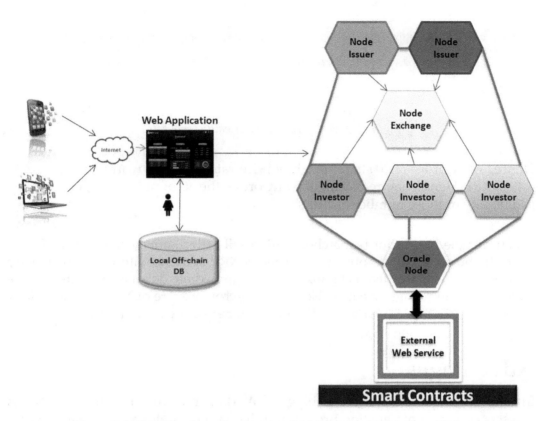

Figure 5.1: How Ripple can be integrated with R3 Corda distributed ledger

Here, instead of the tokenization model, we use real-time payment by individual buyers. All buyers and sellers need to create an XRP account on XRP Ledger, which must be validated during the registration process to get an entry into the auction system.

Forex rates

Before placing any buy order, the XRP account information can be verified for number of XRPs available. Also, the forex rate from USD (or any other fiat currency) to XRP can be calculated from many APIs, exposed publicly on the internet.

For example, as shown in *Figure 5.2*, https://min-api.cryptocompare.com/data/pric ehistorical?fsym=USD&tsyms=XRP gives you the latest forex rate, which was 2.46 as of June 9, 2019.

Figure 5.2: Web service for retrieving forex rates

Hence, a buy order of 20 shares at a buy price/rate of $100 is worth $100 \times 20 \times 2.46$ = 4920 XRP. Hence, before placing the buy order, the account has to be checked for availability of those number of XRPs.

Whenever the buy order is matched with a sell order, money can be transferred from the buyer's XRP account to the seller's XRP account within approximately four seconds, and the deal is finalized by the immediate delivery of shares on the ledger of the exchange. We can also use the escrow feature of XRP Ledger to lock some XRPs from the buyer as a collateral even before the auction starts.

Advantages

Instant settlement is the next big thing. [3] Working on two very innovative Swiss projects and one gold auction project in India with the golden combination of R3 Corda and Ripple (Corda Settler) has revealed so much interest in the market in this space. Canada-based GuildOne, who is launching **Energy Block Exchange (EBX)**, has tested Corda Settler for its platform and has found it performing efficiently. [4] Some of the key benefits of using Ripple are as follows:

- It will cut down the settlement time drastically from days and hours to seconds.

- The risks related to fluctuations in the price of XRP against any currency are minimized as auction occurs for a small time period and the exchange happens in real time.

- A buyer can push more money into the XRP account by converting fiat currency to XRP and can place as many buy orders as needed.

- The exchange can even ask the buyers to deposit certain amount of XRPs as a collateral to safeguard the auction process and enhance the performance of matching by retaining only valid participants. Post auction the exchange can return those XRPs to the buyer using XRP Ledger's partial payment feature so that the exchange does not have to bear the transaction fee.

- Traders from different countries and operating on different international currencies can participate in this auction as all the payments can be handled by XRP Ledger after converting the currencies to XRP.

- You can also use XRP Ledger's issued currencies feature for auction, where parties from different countries operate on different currencies.

Please note that though this can also be achieved by connecting to the SWIFT gpi network, SWIFT is usually more time-consuming. Transactions on SWIFT gpi mostly take around thirty minutes or more, which would not be suitable for instant settlement business models. Also, SWIFT is much more expensive than Ripple.

Summary

In this chapter, we covered the following topics:

- Limitations in e-Auctions
- Different solution models and how they can help
- Solution architecture for instant settlement with Ripple
- Advantages of introducing Ripple

References

1. Session Timings -https://www.bseindia.com/markets/equity/session_timings.aspx?expandable=0.

2. Addressing liquidity challenges in T+2 securities settlement - https://www.bankingtech.com/2018/03/addressing-liquidity-challenges-in-t2-securities-settlement/

3. Instant Settlement: Disbursements Next Big Thing - https://www.pymnts.com/digital-payments/2019/ingo-money-instant-settlement-merchant-sales/

4 . R3 and GuildOne Announce Inclusion of Manual Settlement on Corda Settler - https://guild1.co/2019/06/19/r3-and-guildone-announce-inclusion-of-manual-settlement-on-corda-settler/

Chapter 6

Use Case: Settlement for Intraday Trading in Money Market

In this chapter, we will discuss the different types of financial markets and focus on money market, which works mainly on liquidity. We will review a use case where there is a requirement of intraday money transfers and instant settlement. This kind of business model was never possible before, the sole reason being that the existing settlement time in most part of the world is T+1, T+2, or even T+3 days. However, using Ripple we can reduce this time to less than four seconds. Let's find out how.

Investment in finance is an indispensable part of any country's economy. Be it stocks, bonds, derivatives, or currencies, we all invest in one form or another to get higher interest than regular saving. As shown in *Figure 6.1* below, the Indian financial market is largely divided into different segments, namely, capital market, money market, and commodities market.

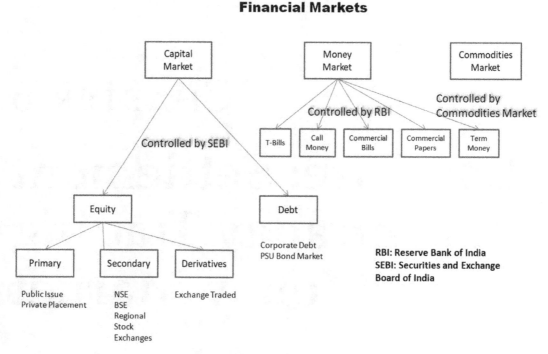

Figure 6.1: Types of Indian financial markets

Capital market

In a capital market, people invest in different financial instruments such as stocks, bonds, and debentures for a long duration of time, mostly for years together. Usually money invested in a capital market is the amount that the investor does not need on an immediate basis.

Money market

Money market on the other hand is just the opposite where individuals or organizations lend or borrow for a short duration ranging from a few hours up to less than a year. Some of the money market use cases are promissory notes, bills of exchange, commercial paper, T bill, call money, and so on.

Why is a strong money market important for intraday trading?

We are all aware how lack of liquidity in banks led to the banking crisis in the USA in 2007–08. The aftereffects were drop in house prices, loss of employment, and panic among funders all over the world, thus halting investment and growth. This was one of the greatest recessions of documented human history that continued for a long period and has been a great learning for financial advisors as well as central banks.

Since then, many governments and central banks have revised and reformed financial policies and made it mandatory for banks to hold much higher liquidity buffers. The **internal capital adequacy assessment process (ICAAP)** and the **internal liquidity adequacy assessment process (ILAAP)** are two such policies devised by the **European Central Bank (ECB)** for financial organizations operating in the EU territory. As per ECB, "Ensure that institutions have robust strategies, policies, processes and systems for the . . . management and monitoring of liquidity risk . . . including intraday . . . to ensure that institutions maintain adequate levels of liquidity buffers". European countries today are emphasizing on liquidity for intraday trading and day-to-day operations, as they have realized how a strong money market can reduce the risk for banks under stressed condition.

Challenges in money market

Intraday trading is a special kind of money market trading where borrowers that are often banks or financial organizations borrow large amounts of money for a small duration of time and return it to the lender bank or financial institution within the same day with interest. The participants in this money market might be banks based in different countries and working in different currencies.

Most of the money market trading, especially intraday trading, happens over the counter. Some of the issues that intraday trading faces are as follows:

- Real-time trading and settlement

- Settlement time in processing of money transfer

- Currency exchange

Business scenario

Consider the below scenario of a typical money market intraday business flow:

- Bank A sends out a **request for quote (RFQ)** to counterparties, requesting an offer for a period of four hours in USD.

- Bank A receives three offers back and selects the cheapest of these.

- Bank A confirms the trade to Bank B (the lender).

- Bank B transfers the cash to Bank A via Settler for a four-hour period.

- Bank A transfers the cash back to Bank B with accumulated interest after four hours.

Presently no settlement system exists for intraday trading in money market in any part of the world. If we consider Europe, the payments from different financial organizations are geared around TARGET2, a **real-time gross settlement (RTGS)** system owned and operated by the Eurosystem. For banks and financial organizations in need of quick settlement, the lowest duration for intraday business scenarios is one day overnight. In such scenarios, Ripple/XRP can offer instant settlement solution.

Complete Blockchain solution

Figure 6.2 below shows a complete decentralized architecture where each financial organization is represented as a node on the Blockchain network. Each organization can have its own XRP account that it can provide during its offline registration process and can be saved to the off-chain database.

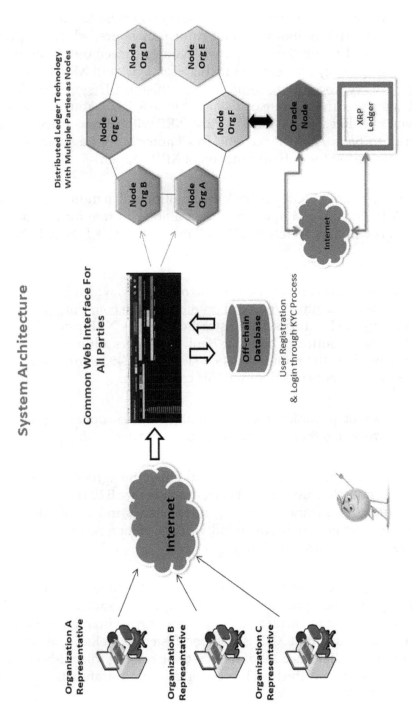

Figure 6.2: Architecture for instant settlement in intraday trading

During the time of trading, Bank B (the lender) will need to transfer the required amount (let's say $100 million) to Bank A for four hours, which is specified in a contract. So, first through the oracle node, you can reach out to an external web service for the currency conversion rate between USD and XRP. For this example, https://min-api.cryptocompare.com/data/pricehistorical?fsym=USD&tsyms=XRP was used, which returned a rate of 2.49 as of June 6, 2019. You can use some other API that you may like. So, 100 million × 2.49 XRP will be transferred from Bank B's XRP account to Bank A's XRP account. In Chapter 3, we have already discussed how to transfer using the submit function of XRP Ledger.

After four hours, Bank A will pay back the amount with a mutually agreed interest rate to Bank B. For this example, consider the interest rate for the loan to be 4%. Hence, Bank A will have to return 100 million × 2.49 × (1 + 1.04) XRP back to Bank B.

Now Bank B can convert this back to its own currency, which is USD here. At this moment let's say that https://min-api.cryptocompare.com/data/pricehistorical?fsym=USD&tsyms=XRP returns 2.48 instead of 2.49, as XRP price fluctuations are possible. So, the amount of USD that Bank B receives ultimately after currency conversion would be 100 million × 2.49 × (1 + 1.04)/2.48. Conversion charges and other minor fees are not considered in this calculation.

This model can help banks from different countries operating with different currencies to work together, thus boosting business across the globe.

One may wonder, what if Bank A does not return the agreed amount to Bank B? Well, one must note that money market transactions are B2B transactions occurring between reputed organizations with a verified history and are administered under strict regulation rather than between individuals. Hence, rest assured that nobody can run away with the traded money!

Intraday trading is a classic example that can greatly benefit from the integration of decentralized technologies like Corda and Ripple through Oracle services. Now you may ask why we can't achieve this by integrating with regular SWIFT gpi. We have already discussed that XRP is cheaper, faster, and eliminates the need for a nostro account that dictates a lot of money to be staying idle without investment. SWIFT gpi takes around thirty minutes for clearing a transaction, which is also unsuitable for intraday scenario.

Advantages

Advantages of using Ripple are pretty much the same as discussed previously. In fact, thanks to higher need of liquidity, Ripple could be a blessing for money market as well as any international intraday business where there is a need of instant settlement.

Summary

In this chapter, we covered the following topics:

- Different types of financial markets

- Money market and its challenges

- Ripple solution architecture for intraday trading and quick settlement

- Advantages of introducing Ripple

References

1. Instimatch Intraday/Money-market solution - https://marketplace.r3.com/solutions/instimatch-intradaymoney-market-solution

2. Should there be Intraday Money Markets? - https://www.newyorkfed.org/medialibrary/media/research/staff_reports/sr337.pdf

CHAPTER 7

Use Case: Derivatives and Swaps

In this chapter, we will broadly cover the different types of derivative instruments available in the finance market and how adoption of Ripple can make it a much more profitable business.

Derivative is a financial contract between two (or more) different parties for a future transaction whose value is determined on the basis of an underlying asset. The transaction could be for any type of asset such as equity, indices, commodities, cash, or any other valuables. The basic purpose of any type of derivative is to hedge the risk related to investments, and hence it is widely used by business houses.

Types of derivatives

As shown in *Figure 7.1* below, a financial derivative could be of many different types addressing the different hedging needs of individuals or organizations participating in the trading.

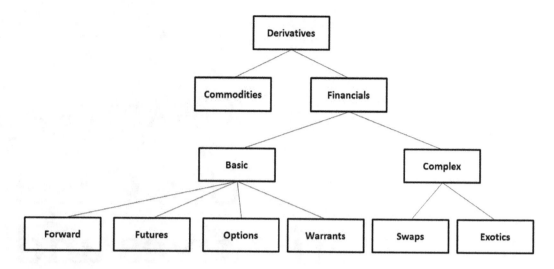

Figure 7.1: Types of derivatives

Forward

Forward is a type of contract where the parties agree to buy and sell an underlying asset at a fixed price on a predetermined future date. Depending upon the price fluctuation of the commodity, either the buyer or the seller profits from this trading.

Futures

Like forward, in a future contract too parties agree for trading at a future date and time on a pre-agreed quantity and price. Futures are traded on exchanges with involvement of a clearing house, thus minimizing the risk of defaulting. Forward contracts, on the other hand, are private agreements between parties to buy and sell an asset at a specified price in the future. Hence, there is a possibility of one or more parties to default. Hence, the risk is higher.

Options

Options are again like forwards where two parties sign a contract for a trade at a future date. The only difference is that the owner of the option, be it buyer or seller, is under no obligation to commit the trade. In case trade does not get committed, only the amount invested in the option is lost.

Warrants

Warrants are long-term options where the maturity period is longer than a year.

Swaps

Unlike others, swap can occur as a series of forward derivatives, e.g., *interest rate swapping* where two parties agree to swap a fixed interest rate with a variable interest rate. Hence, what follows is a series of cash flows in the future. Interest rate, forex, and equity swaps are the most frequently used swaps in the financial markets.

Challenges in derivatives

One thing is common among all these derivative types, that there are more than one organization or parties who wish to do a transaction at a future date at a predetermined price. The complexity of this transaction is far greater if the participating parties are from different countries and operate in more than one global currency.

It's worth mentioning that interest rate swaps are the single largest type of derivatives in today's world, making up more than 80% of the value of all derivative contracts signed by US commercial banks. Now, let's consider this specific scenario of currency swap that is pretty prevalent in financial markets where two counterparties agree on exchanging their rates on a predetermined day and time. Usually such swaps occur on the basis of LIBOR rates or **forex** rates or some sort of base rate. Additionally, these swaps can be of two types:

- Single currency interest rate swap

- Different currency swap

Let's consider the use case of World Bank and IBM, known as the earliest currency and interest rate swap deal that occurred between IBM and World Bank in 1981. It's shown in *Figure 7.2*:

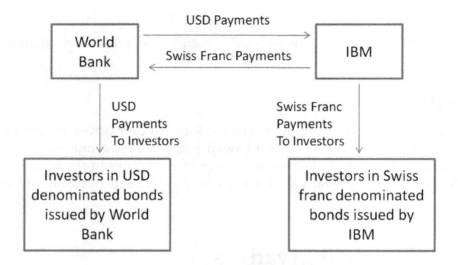

Figure 7.2: First official forex swap between World Bank and IBM in 1981

The World Bank in that time period needed to borrow Swiss francs and German marks. However, it had already reached its upper limit and was banned from borrowing more from those countries. At the same time IBM, which already had a huge chunk of reserve in those aforementioned currencies, was in need of dollars from the USA where lending prices were too high. So, as suggested by Solomon Brothers, one of the most well-known banks of that era, World Bank and IBM exchanged their currencies with a swap deal. This first global derivative scenario opened the gates for similar transactions in global corporations. Such deals bypassed national capital controls and shielded organizations from currency fluctuations, boosting international trading to the next level.

Solution

Currency swaps today still have limitations especially for unusual currency pairs, thus prohibiting derivative business, as the availability of such currencies and their price fluctuation pose a major risk for reserves. In such cases, we can still do the swap with the help of Ripple/XRP with a predetermined price of currencies regardless of the fluctuations in XRP. Basically, if you want to get the closest bid-ask spread in forex on unusual currency pairs, you need market makers. Ripple can show several different pathways of getting the best prices as it does in spot forex, thus reducing the cost of these swaps. No need to mention that the huge fees for currency exchange and middleman-ship can be completely sidelined in such scenarios.

Consider the following scenario:

- Adams Food Chain, a fast food organization in Spain, wishes to open a few branches in Argentina. For doing so, it needs a certain amount of funds in Pesos, Argentina's local currency.

- However, we all know that Peso is one of the most unstable currencies, and hence the food chain does not wish to reserve a lot of them in one go.

- Instead, it will exchange the currencies against its Euros at certain time intervals.

- Similarly, Bank of Argentina wishes to procure Euros in exchange of Pesos from Adams Food Chain as the Euro is considered to be relatively more stable as a currency.

- So, they can enter a swap deal to swap currencies on the first of every month at a particular forex rate.

- Now Adams Food Chain considers USD as the most stable global currency, and hence can do some spot trading and secure USD in exchange of some Euros. So, Adams Food Chain can exchange USD for Euros just in time (morning of first of every month) and do the swapping on time so that the chances of loss by rate fluctuation can be minimized.

Advantages

Advantages of using Ripple in international derivative scenarios are countless. Some are listed below; however, it's up to business leaders to come up with more options.

- Thanks to low fees of exchange, XRP can be of great use in forex swaps.

- Settlement time of less than four seconds can lead to just-in-time payment, and there is no need to hold the money in any particular currency for long.

- Investors have the option of trading with other currencies and earn until the last moment of payment.

- Ripple allows trading in almost all fiat and crypto currencies; hence options of trading are far more with Ripple adoption.

Summary

In this chapter, we covered the following topics:

- Different types of derivatives

- Challenges in derivatives in international space

- Ripple solution

- Advantages of introducing Ripple

CHAPTER 8

Use Case: Trade Finance

In this chapter, we will discuss one of the most crucial use case of trade finance and, with an example, discuss how Ripple can reduce risks related to the entire life cycle through its superior features of partial payment and escrow.

What is trade finance?

Trade finance is a term often used in case of international business among importers and exporters.

Trade finance is the lifeline of global trade as 80%–90% of the world trade system is reliant upon it, which is worth around $10 trillion per annum. In 2017 alone, $15.5 trillion worth of merchandise exports were transported around the world across sea, air, rail, and road, and also needed financing.

Use Case: Petroleum trade

Let's say Petrolux Ltd, an energy wholesaler and distributor company in India, wishes to import a huge amount of petroleum from a reputed oil company, Black Gold Services, in Saudi Arabia. Black Gold Services has tie-up with numerous crude oil extractor organizations from where petroleum is brought for exporting to the outside world. Now this oil can be imported in many different ways such as through Arabic Sea in ships, or through large goods carrier vehicles on road.

Sometimes high value items are also transferred through cargo airlines. This transport time can be very high depending upon the location in India where the oil reaches. The energy distributor in India needs to be regularly updated on the location of the goods as it travels towards the destination. Once the oil reaches the destination, it has to be further transported to different petrol pumps across India.

The typical participants in the entire business cycle can be as follows:

- Oil importer/buyer

- Oil exporter/seller

- Oil extractors attached to seller

- Retailers attached to buyer

- Store houses

- Refinery

- Transport organizations

- Ports of shipment

- Government authorities for approval of trading

In reality, this list can be much bigger, but only some of the participants are shown in *Figure 8.1* for this use case.

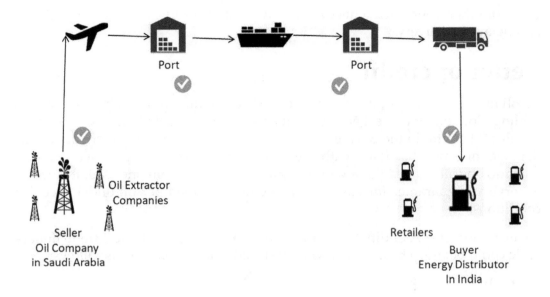

Figure 8.1: Participants in trade finance

Trade finance is a special type supply chain trading system that occurs between parties working in different countries and regions. Hence, this brings much more complexity to a delivery against payment system, as there might be no common rules and regulations between the participating organizations and there is no central party who can control the entire process. Also, the parties might be working with different currencies whose exchange values might vary throughout the entire cycle of trade finance, which could be months if not years. In spite of all the odds, this trading system has been prevalent for thousands of years, bearing with many different kinds of risks and hurdles.

Mitigating manufacturing and payment risks

Trade finance helps to mitigate risks associated with international trading by introducing different tools and more parties to the entire business.

Getting business insured

It's highly advisable to get your business insured, especially when the business is between developing countries. There are possibilities of certain political events affecting or even completely jeopardizing operations by suppliers, manufacturing units, or others. Such incidents can negatively affect tariffs, leading to trade bans and delays in delivery.

Letter of credit

Involving banks early in the business cycle is a common practice in international trading. Both buyer and seller organizations collaborate with banks who work on behalf of them to do the payment if there is any delay, no-show, theft, accidental damage, or any other issue with the shipment or quality of products. In such scenarios, a *letter of credit* or a written contract is issued from one bank to another to serve as a guarantee for payments made to a specified person under specified conditions.

So, in reality, the list of different parties who participate in a typical trade finance cycle could be much bigger than what we listed before. Some are as follows:

- Buyer's bank

- Seller's bank

- Funders and loan providers (to buyer)

- Insurers

- Credit agencies for evaluating credit risks in trade

- Many other service providers

Business process flow

The entire business process can be broadly described as follows:

1. Buyer from India and Seller from London mutually agree to do some delivery against payment trading that involves shipping of deliverables among different countries.

2. Buyer gets connected to some bank in India for a **letter of credit** (**LoC**).

3. The issuing bank prepares and sends the LoC to Bank of Arabia (termed as seller bank or advising bank).

4. The advising/seller bank does verification and discusses the same with Seller for any modification.

5. There is a cycle here between both banks and Buyer and Seller until the LoC is finalized.

6. In the meantime, both Buyer and Seller reach out to insurance companies for getting them protected against deliveries as well as payments.

7. Seller organization sends instructions to all its attached oil extracting organizations to deliver a certain amount of oil by a particular date.

8. Once the required amount of oils reaches Seller, it's refined in factories and then shipped.

9. The shipment takes a huge amount of time, and goods travel port by port to finally reach the destination.

10. On delivery, Seller receives a delivery confirmation document. Seller provides that delivery confirmation receipt to the advising/seller bank.

11. The advising bank dispatches the receipt to Buyer/issuing bank.

12. The issuing bank verifies the delivery as per contract, and if everything is fine then pays to the advising bank.

13. The issuing bank transfers the payment to Seller as agreed and keeps their commission.

14. Buyer, who is a wholesaler, transfers petroleum to all distributors and retailers.

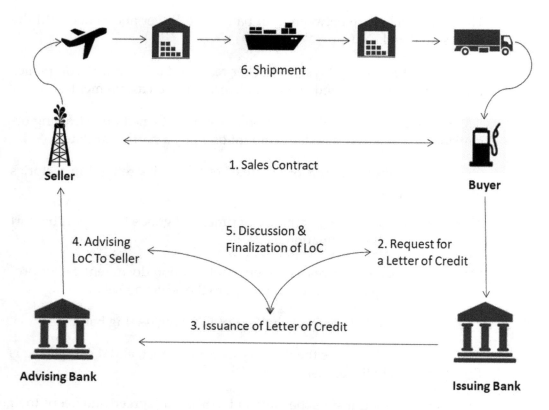

Figure 8.2: Processes in trade finance

However, in reality, many of the involved parties could ask for pre-payment. A few examples are given below:

- The seller might ask for 10% down payment as soon as the contract is signed between the parties.

- The seller might also ask for another 20% advance on completion of manufacturing or at the initiation of dispatching the order.

- The oil extractors may ask for 20% pre-payment from the seller before delivering the oil.

Challenges in international trading

Although trade finance is a much complex version of delivery against payment, in practice it's far riskier for many different reasons, the most difficult area being payment.

Parties

Of the parties that participate in the entire cycle, many might be first-timers, or working with each other for the first time and hence completely unknown to each other. In such a case, background verification and on-time payment could be huge challenges.

Currency

The buyers, seller, banks, insurers, and rest of the parties that participate in the entire cycle of trade might be from different countries and operating in different local currencies. Hence, conversion of currencies and speed of payment is always an issue, as well as the price fluctuations of the currencies.

Payment

Delay in payment can jeopardize the entire system. As there is no central system, it's one of the weakest areas for trade finances. Also, the considerable time taken by the clearing houses in the international market using the SWIFT network is not business savvy.

Solution

Using RippleNet, investor guarantee can be established via cash collateral, often held in a time-held escrow account on XRP Ledger. Now let's consider the following scenario:

- Let's say a deal has been finalised between Petrolux Ltd, the buyer, and Black Gold Services, the seller in Saudi Arabia, for $100 million.

- Both parties have agreed for a pre-payment of 10% from the buyer to the seller as soon as a contract is signed. So Petrolux Ltd converts $10 million worth INR to XRP as per that day's forex rates and pays to the XRP account of Black Gold Services using transaction type **Payment**. The latter can convert the XRPs to Saudi Riyal.

- Petrolux Ltd can also pay the amount as a check on XRP Ledger by using transaction type **CheckCreate** with a maximum expiry date.

- At the last moment if Petrolux Ltd realizes there's a mistake in the contract, they can cancel the check using **ChequeCancel** transaction type.

- Black Gold Services connects to five of its oil extractor parties and pays each 10% advance and gets the process started. If he has received through an XRP check, he can withdraw money using transaction type **CheckCash.**

- Once all the required oil is ready for export, the delivery is audited by the buyer's surveyor and another 20% of the entire worth ($20 million), which was held in the buyer's escrow account for the seller, is released. This escrow was created by invoking **EscrowCreate** transaction type on XRP Ledger with a time-held condition.

- Once the shipment reaches India, another 10% of the amount again held in the buyer's escrow account for the seller is released.

- Finally, when the shipment reaches the destination within agreed time and clears quality regulation, the final chunk of 60% held in escrow accounts is released.

- However, in the entire process, if the seller or its oil extractor parties fail to fulfill conditions of time or quality, then the buyer can cancel the amount held in escrow and it would return to him.

Advantages

For many reasons Ripple's XRP Ledger seems to be the number one choice among its contemporaries.

- Escrow services can be of great relief to all parties involved on the seller side as money in escrow accounts is assured to be released on delivery of goods.

- Ripple reduces the overall time of settlement from days to a few seconds.

- There is reduced risk of currency fluctuation. Payment can be agreed upon as per the date and time of delivery and as per the rate of international currency exchange at that time, which XRP Ledger can find out on the spot.

- Fraud is brought under control as all parties are on the same page and any discrepancy could be easily shared between the concerned or all parties in real time.

- Financial transparency is established for all the participating parties.

Complete Blockchain solution

Although we can integrate Ripple with our traditional applications that are based on central servers, using a complete Blockchain solution would be an ideal solution here. As we already discussed, international trading is a true example of distributed system where we have multiple entities working under different countries with varying rules and regulations. In *Figure 8.3* below, you can find some of the participants represented by nodes. An independent node, i.e., the oracle node, connects to external web services for forex and payment in Ripple XRP.

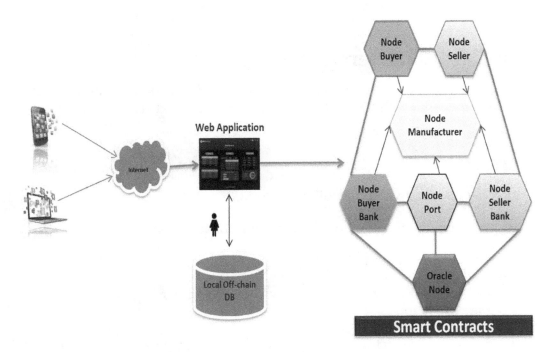

Figure 8.3: All participants represented on decentralized ledger

This figure is configured with Corda Settler (i.e., R3 Corda + Ripple), but you can use any other Blockchain platform of your choice.

Live Use Case

Ripple is equally famous among banks, payment providers, as well as international finance. Some of the latest developments in this area are as follows:

Euro Exim Bank

As per a news report in January 2019, [1] Euro Exim bank, an innovative global financial institution that caters to a range of trade finance instruments such as instant letters of credit, corporate bank accounts (Prestige Plus), letters of credit, stand-by letters of credit, international wire transfers, bank guarantees, prepaid Mastercards, and trade credit lines is pilot testing Ripple's enterprise products xCurrent and xRapid.

Standard Chartered Bank

Much before Euro Exim, a similar attempt was made by the Standard Chartered Bank in association with **Bank of Singapore** (**DBS**) to tackle trade finance. [2]

Summary

In this chapter, we covered the following topics:

- Working model of international trading with example

- Challenges in international trade finance

- Features of Ripple such as escrow, checks, and partial payments and how they can help

- Solution architecture of Ripple and how it can be used in international trading space

- Advantages of introducing Ripple

- Complete Blockchain solution

References

1. Ripple and Euro Exim to trial new Blockchain-based trade finance capability for xCurrent - https://www.gtreview.com/news/fintech/ripple-and-euro-exim-to-trial-new-blockchain-based-trade-finance-capability-for-xcurrent/

2. How Standard Chartered is using Ripple to rethink trade finance - https://www.coindesk.com/how-standard-chartered-is-using-ripple-to-rethink-trade-finance

Some other great resources for reference are as follows:

1. Can Blockchain make Trade Finance more inclusive - https://www.r3.com/wp-content/uploads/2018/07/Can-Blockchain-Make-Trade-Finance-More-Inclusive-1.pdf

2. Use Case - Trade Finance Letter of Credit - https://wiki.hyperledger.org/requirements/use-cases/use-case-trade-finance-letter-of-credit

3. Letters of Credit Network - https://github.com/hyperledger/composer-sample-networks/tree/master/packages/letters-of-credit-network

4. Letter of Credit Demo Corda - https://github.com/corda/LetterOfCredit

5. Trade Finance and Blockchain three essential Case Studies - http://cib.db.com/insights-and-initiatives/flow/trade_finance_and_the_blockchain_three_essential_case_studies.htm

6. How Letter of Credit works - https://www.thebalance.com/how-letters-of-credit-work-315201

7. HSBC, ING Bank execute Blockchain transaction with Reliance Industries - https://telecom.economictimes.indiatimes.com/news/hsbc-ing-bank-execute-blockchain-transaction-with-reliance-industries/66505747

8. Voltron, a Blockchain-Based Trade Finance Platform, Edges Closer to Real-World Use - https://www.nasdaq.com/article/voltron-a-blockchain-based-trade-finance-platform-edges-closer-to-real-world-use-cm1052724

CHAPTER 9
Stablecoins

When discussing Ripple, it would be unfair to not cover some of its competitors that are also gaining popularity as alternate payment mechanisms. In this chapter, we will discuss Stablecoins, special kind of crypto currencies that some of the banks are adopting instead of Ripple.

What are Stablecoins?

One of the top reasons for most crypto currencies in the world, including Bitcoin, always being criticized is they are not backed up by any collateral. For explaining this further, let's recall Chapter 1 where we discussed the history of money and payment. Starting from barter system to the digital era, currency has undergone several changes. Be it crops, gold, silver, spices, or salt, currency has been used as the medium of exchange and has always had an inherent value associated with it. With paper money, the issue of trust came into picture, and banks as well as governments came forward to establish that trust.

However, in order to bring the same barter-system-like democracy to the exchange of valuables that was prevalent in ancient times (i.e., before paper money), and also to get rid of the middleman charges imposed by banks, Stablecoins were introduced. But hey, was Ripple not conceptualized with the same purpose? Well, the biggest issue with Ripple that deters financial institutions from adopting it wholeheartedly is the price fluctuation. In fact, this is true for most crypto currencies. Who has not heard of the rags to riches (and back to rags) story of Bitcoin? In *Figure 9.1,* you can see how the price of XRP has varied against USD since 2014, which can be a concern for certain business models.

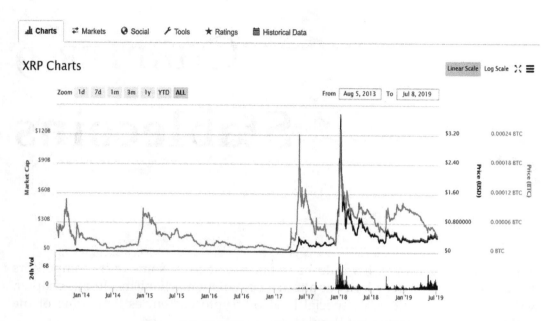

Figure 9.1: Price fluctuation in XRP against USD

If organizations need all the benefits of Ripple without falling into the volatile crypto trap, they can create their new business model — Stablecoins. These are new type of crypto currencies created through the same tokenization model, but they are backed by real-world securities owing to which their price remains relatively unaltered.

Types of Stablecoins

The size of Stablecoin market currently is close to $3 billion, i.e., 2.7% of the total market value of all crypto assets. [1] As per the collateral used in creating the Stablecoin, they can be divided into four categories: backed by fiat currency, backed by valuable collaterals, backed by crypto currency, and not backed by any collateral. [2]

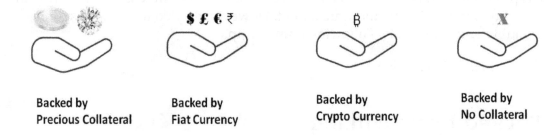

Backed by	Backed by	Backed by	Backed by
Precious Collateral	Fiat Currency	Crypto Currency	No Collateral

Figure 9.2: Types of Stablecoins

Backed by valuable collaterals

We will discuss the use of this kind of collateral in the next chapter. Such coins are stable and trustworthy and can be converted to tokens for further use. However, they are centralized and need auditing. Some of the examples are as follows:

- Backed by diamonds: diamDexx

- Backed by gold: **Digix Gold (DGX)**

- Backed by Swiss real estate: **SwissRealCoin (SRC)**

Backed by fiat currency

Tether is the first Stablecoin in this category and represents 98% of the market cap of all Stablecoins today. It's backed by USD. Fiat-backed Stablecoins are relatively stable as they have the authority of the government. However, they are centralized, require trust, and need strong regulation and auditing. Below are a few more fiat-backed Stablecoins:

- Backed by USD: Tether, USD Coin, True USD, PAX, and DAI

- Backed by Euro: Stasis

- Backed by GBP: BGBP

Backed by crypto currency

Crypto-currency-backed Stablecoins are decentralized in consensus, high in liquidity, super efficient, and transparent. However, they come at the cost of high volatility and complexity. Following is an example:

- MakerDAO (DAI)

Backed by no collateral

In this category, the Stablecoins are created backed by an algorithm to create and maintain currencies totally dependent on demand and supply to keep the value of the currency constant. They are decentralized and stable, but pretty complex and not so popular yet.

As shown in *Figure 9.3*, all these Stablecoins have their pros and cons and it's up to the organization to use one over another.

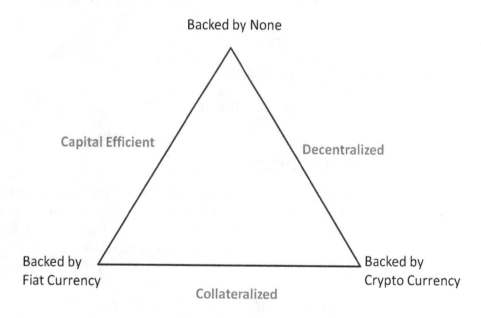

Figure 9.3: Pros and cons of different types of Stablecoins [3]

Most popular Stablecoins of the world

Now let's discuss some of the most popular Stablecoins in the world irrespective of the categories they fall into.

Tether

Tether, also known as Realcoin in the beginning, followed by USDT, is a Stablecoin originally issued with 1:1 ratio with USD; in other words, for one Tether coin, its issuer organization Tether Ltd claimed to have reserve of one USD. This currency initially issued in October 2014 raised too many expectations, making it the most widely used Stablecoin as of June 2019. However, recently critics started pushing the issuer for a close audit and submission of reports showcasing proof of enough USD reserves as a backup for all the virtual coins, but Tether has failed to do so and has ended up as one of the most controversial crypto currencies. Lately Tether has started representing Euro as well.

JPM Coin: A Stablecoin by JPMorgan

Of the entire list of Stablecoins today, JPM Coin is perhaps the most talked about virtual currency. As announced by the American multinational investment bank, JPMorgan Chase, it's the second Stablecoin to be backed by USD again in the same 1:1 ratio of value. However, with time it would also be used against other fiat currencies. The sole purpose of JPMorgan to enable **real-time gross settlement (RTGS)** between institutional clients and establish this new virtual currency was to address the same issue as Ripple — facilitating *international remittance* without the price volatility of Ripple XRP (But note that one can use Ripple's xCurrent without using XRP). With the use of JPM Coin, the transaction settlement time between JPMorgan and its clients in international remittance scenarios has now reduced to seconds.

The entire process of international remittance for JPM Coin involves three steps:

1. A client of any JPMorgan bank deposits amount in fiat currency (currently USD) to a designated account and receives an equivalent number of JPM Coins in exchange.

2. These JPM Coins are used for transactions over Quorum Blockchain network with other JPMorgan clients.

3. Holders of JPM Coins redeem them for USD at some other JPMorgan bank anywhere in world.

This entire process, which used to take up to two days, can now be completed in a few seconds.

According to the JPMorgan investor day slide, 185+ banks have signed a **letter of intent (LoI)** to use JPM Coin. While the banking industry all over the world went berserk after this news, as per Ripple's CEO, it would not be of much value as all big banks would start creating their own currencies leading to interoperability issues. He also added that JPM Coin has value only within its network; it can never be a competitor to Ripple. Also, hey, is tokenization really needed when we already have a crypto currency with such a grand solution for payment available on a global network on the Blockchain platform?

JPM Coin, which runs on private-permissioned ledger, Quorum (a fork on Ethereum public Blockchain), is still in prototype phase but is testing most of the clearing processes of the bank and might go into production soon. It has a long-term vision of building a platform ecosystem (perhaps by using this product) for finding solutions to complex processes such as KYC, onboarding, errors, returns, and so on.

Libra: A Stablecoin by Facebook

On June 18, 2019, Facebook unveiled its plan to launch a new crypto currency called Libra in 2020. This magnificent effort by Facebook is backed by twenty-eight founding members including Visa, Mastercard, PayPal, Uber, Lyft, Coinbase, and a couple of other industry leaders. Facebook is having continuing discussion with all its allies to raise about $1 billion in total as collateral for the Stablecoin to buffer it against volatility from financial services supporting Libra.

Earlier, the *Wall Street Journal* reported that Facebook has been working for over a year now to launch a Stablecoin-based payments platform. People can use this Blockchain-based solution to send and receive money to and from people across the world and can do online purchases. However, they can still see the money in their wallet in local or fiat currency.

Let's explore how Libra works.

1. User signs up to Facebook's Calibra wallet after identity checks.

2. User links bank account.

3. User uses local currency of that country to buy Libra tokens.

4. User transfers Libra tokens to another user in text message type function or pays a merchant for some purchase.

5. The recipient can convert Libra to local currency or can store it for purchase from other merchants or money transfer.

6. In future, Facebook will roll out the Libra payment platform to stores.

7. Money held by Libra will be backed by low-volatility assets such as deposits, government bonds, and major currencies.

Please read the Libra whitepaper [4] to know more.

Some of the attractive features of Libra are as follows:

- It's a low-volatility crypto currency with very low fees for money transfer.

- The project is non-profit.

- Although it was started on a permissioned Blockchain platform, gradually it has vision to become permission-less to reach the masses.

- It offers interoperability by supporting major currencies.

Through this project, Facebook wishes to reach the unbanked — numerous people around the world — for whom basic financial services are still out of reach and also aims to eliminate the swipe and card processing fees, generally around 2%–3%, paid by merchants to banks and payment networks for every transaction. If it's successful, it would bring a new revolution to the global payment system. In my view, it's a positive mission by Facebook, and it's hard to argue on its drawbacks especially for society. However, when it comes to their vision of *global money*, it may raise many eyebrows as many entities and regulators might not like the idea of a BigTech moving into the lucrative business of printing money. Needless to say, the social media giant might first focus on the Indian market as it's the prime market in the world to receive maximum international remittances.

One might wonder, what is Ripple's take on this new development in the world of crypto currencies? Well, Ripple CEO Brad Garlinghouse is unfazed by Libra, as

Libra is not market-ready yet, whereas international remittance is an area where Ripple is already engaged since past seven to eight years and has almost invaded it. Also, according to Brad, Facebook and Ripple are targeting different markets. Ripple focuses on large-scale settlement with banks, whereas this Facebook product is focused on retail market. However, (perhaps) as a backup plan, Ripple is investing a whopping $50 million in a strategic partnership with remittance giant MoneyGram.

Stablecoin by Swiss Stock Exchange

The **Swiss Stock Exchange** (SIX) has asked its central bank to issue a new Stablecoin, as per a news report in June 2019. [5]

The new fiat-based digital exchange of SIX called SDX is a new tokenized currency that, with the help of distributed ledger technology, will help in bridging the gap between traditional finance and the growing world of crypto assets. This new platform of SDX will perform tasks such as atomic swaps of tokenized securities and other assets on Blockchain.

The best part of this project is that all the current operations of the exchange, such as equities, fixed income, and funds, can be tokenized within a Blockchain environment, leading to more automation and instant settlement. The whole process will be executed under the same regulatory oversight as the existing exchange services.

The testing part of this project has already initiated, with a possible go-live early next year.

Stablecoin by Binance

Global crypto exchange Binance too has confirmed the launch of its own Stablecoin sometime soon. This new crypto currency, known as Binance GBP, will be backed by the British pound.

Ripple versus Stablecoins— who will win?

So far, we have discussed the different products of Ripple and how they can be used, through different use cases. At the same time, we also learnt what are Stablecoins and some of the examples in business models. So, if someone asks you which one you would choose for your business, you would definitely be tempted to say "Stablecoin." After all who does not love the surety of investments with Stablecoins especially if backed by some collateral? However, the answer is not that simple. Let's discuss some of the pros and cons of both products as of June 2019.

Pros of Ripple

- It's high in market share.

- It's open for all and easy to integrate.

- It's available for use with most of the fiat currencies.

Cons of Ripple

- It's not backed by a collateral.

- It can be volatile in terms of forex rates as price influenced simply by demand and supply in market.

Pros of Stablecoins

- It's backed by a collateral, and hence there is less risk of frequent price fluctuation.

Cons of Stablecoins

- There is no single Stablecoin that can work with all fiat currencies.

- It's difficult for all banks and FinTechs to work on a single Stablecoin. Ultimately, they would all create their own currencies, and interoperability will be another challenge that Ripple has already solved with DLT.

- The organization that issues Stablecoins is not regularly audited to check sufficient reserves of the fiat currency or other collaterals in possession.

- The APIs of Stablecoins are not open source.

With many Stablecoins such as Libra focusing mostly on the retail market and JPM Coin so far confined to its own network, Ripple today seems to be a better option both for B2B and retail business scenarios. The market might work in a very different way when ample Stablecoin options and opportunities come up with lucrative features and well-explained open-source APIs. Until then, we all must wait and watch. In the meantime, let's educate ourselves, do our own research, and not blindly trust certain paid media who can praise or spread fake news on new products. The final decision in choosing the right platform as per the business need of your organization is entirely yours.

Summary

In this chapter, we covered the following topics:

- What are Stablecoins

- Why some banks are adopting them instead of Ripple

- Some very popular Stablecoins in marker: Tether, JPM Coin, and Libra

- Ripple versus Stablecoins

Questions

1. Why are some financial institutions crafting their own Stablecoins instead of adopting Ripple?

    A. Crypto currencies are volatile.

    B. Crypto currencies are expensive.

    C. Crypto currencies can be stolen.

    D. Crypto currencies are banned everywhere.

2. What is the disadvantage of Stablecoins backed by valuables?

   A. Centralized architecture

   B. Need frequent auditing

   C. Both

3. What is the current market capitalization of Stablecoins?

   A. $3 Million

   B. $3 Billion

   C. $3 Trillion

   D. $10 Trillion

4. Which Stablecoin invades the market today?

   A. Tether

   B. Libra

   C. JPM Coin

   D. Digix Gold

5. What is the advantage of Ripple over Stablecoins?

   A. Ripple has already been in production for a long time now, whereas Stablecoins are new.

   B. Stablecoins may face integration challenges with other organizations and countries.

   C. Global currency may have country-specific regulation issues.

   D. All of the above

Answers

1 A, 2 C, 3 B, 4 A, 5 D

References

- Will stablecoins upstage bitcoins? - https://www.livemint.com/market/commodities/will-stablecoins-upstage-bitcoins-1559561098319.html

- Guide to Stablecoin: Types of Stablecoins and Its Importance - https://masterthecrypto.com/guide-to-stablecoin-types-of-stablecoins/

- STABLECOINS TO CHALLENGE MONEY TRANSFERS AND THE DERIVATIVES MARKET? - https://irishtechnews.ie/stablecoins-to-challenge-money-transfers-and-the-derivatives-market/

- Libra White paper - https://libra.org/en-US/white-paper/

- Swiss central bank asked to issue stock exchange digital currency - http://www.swissinfo.ch/eng/latest-news/stablecoin-project_swiss-central-bank-asked-to-issue-stock-exchange-digital-currency/45057590

Some other great resources for reference are as follows:

- There's a *stablecoin invasion* happening. Will this price-stabilized virtual currency be the next big thing to disrupt the crypto space? - https://www.cbinsights.com/research/report/what-are-stablecoins/

- Bitcoinist spoke with Jeremy Dahan, founder and CEO of diamDexx, a diamond-backed stablecoin that promises to make crypto currencies more practical for everyday use - https://bitcoinist.com/diamond-backed-stablecoin-ceo-talks-blockchain-for-storing-value/

- The Rising Stablecoin Market: What purpose do these cryptocurrencies serve? - https://coinfomania.com/what-purpose-do-stablecoins-serve/

- Switzerland's SIX Stock Exchange is working on a Swiss Franc Stablecoin - https://www.coindesk.com/switzerlands-six-stock-exchange-is-working-on-a-swiss-franc-stablecoin

- IMF is bullish on XRP but bearish on Facebook's Libra coin - https://wise-cryptos.com/wise-words/imf-is-bullish-on-xrp-but-bearish-on-facebooks-libra-coin/

CHAPTER 10

Use Case: Islamic Banking

Here, we will discuss how Islamic Finance, a space largely untouched, can benefit from the optimal use of Stablecoins.

What is Islamic banking?

Before jumping to our use case, it's necessary to explain the basics of Islamic Finance and banking to readers, many of whom might be first-timers in this space.

As per *Gulf News* in September 2018, "World Islamic finance market is set to almost double by 2020 from the current $1.81 trillion to $3.25 trillion." As per experts, because of varying standards and regulations, this market is under-explored even today, and yet it has a huge potential for investors.

Islamic banking is a different form of banking adhering to Sharia law based on the Quran and the Hadith. This type of banking is also known as non-interest banking, as Islamic laws prohibit accepting any interest on investment or loans; they consider the interest as a form of money generated by money. So, how do these banks earn profits? Well, they get a share of the profit earned by the borrower. What it means is that, if the borrower is in profit, then the bank is too, or they face the loss together.

There are close to three hundred Islamic banks today spread over fifty-one countries including the USA. Countries like India, which have no Islamic banks, are also considering introducing Islamic windows in standard banks where certain sections of the bank will provide special services as per Sharia law. This is because Muslim population is around 24.1% of the entire world population and their laws make them hesitant and insecure investing in traditional banks. No wonder this is an area that is largely untouched by emerging technologies such as Blockchain and other forms of payment systems.

Crypto currencies in Islamic finance

Just like experts in Asia, Europe, Australia, and Americas, Islamic scholars are also divided on their opinion on accepting crypto currencies in mainstream. Their reason is pretty much similar to what others feel. The general opinion is as follows:

- Crypto currencies are dubious.

- Their price fluctuation is entirely based on demand and supply.

- They mostly lack strong regulations.

- They can be used in money laundering and other criminal activities.

Islamic version of crypto currency

For reasons quoted above, many Islamic countries have declared crypto currencies as un-Islamic and have got them banned. Others have warned citizens not to invest in them even if they are not officially banning them. However, what Islamic finance does allow is usage of crypto currency backed by a real underlying asset, like *gold* or *oil*, which acts as a security token. There are quite a few companies who have created commodity-backed tokens and used it as a crypto or digital currency to hold, buy, and sell products in a specific ecosystem. At the same time, financial instruments such as options, futures, derivatives, and swaps are completely ruled out in Islamic economy.

Scenario: Gold tokenization

Since the beginning of civilization, gold has secured the highest position in the industry as a safe medium of investment for business tycoons around the world. Also, from the Middle East's perspective, gold would be ideal for investment. However, many experts consider gold as dead investment as once purchased we just keep it safe in a locker and forget about it until eternity. Now let's find out how our dead money can offer opportunities for a new world of business by just converting them to tokens of Stablecoins or utility coins.

Let's take the example of **Gold Bar Bank**, which is a bullion bank with loads of gold in reserve. In today's market, the bank delivers gold to many middlemen who are resellers to retailers and sell gold in market at a much higher rate than the purchase rate. Now Gold Bar Bank wishes to create tokens against reserved real gold to use it as an alternate currency in the market. For doing so, it first converts the gold to equivalent number of tokens.

The business scenario would be as follows:

- Gold Bar Bank creates a new decentralized application that would be available in open market for users who can access it from their laptops or download on their mobile device.

- User purchases tokens against real gold from Gold Bar Bank. Payment happens through a payment gateway where the user uses fiat currency of the local country for payment and gets equivalent number of tokens as per that day's exchange rate of gold.

- The bullion bank's decentralized application converts the worth of purchased gold to equivalent virtual tokens and stores those tokens in the user's wallet.

- This decentralized application has many participants who are users or retailers and business owners.

- The user then purchases some product in real world (e.g., buys a cup of coffee from Star Coffee Shop) and searches if Star Coffee Shop is a member of this decentralized application. If yes, then the equivalent tokens would be transferred from the user's wallet to the coffee shop's wallet.

- Now the user wishes to purchase oil from a petrol pump belonging to Arab National Oil Company. If the oil company is not a member of the application, then the application would get connected to an external web service to retrieve that day's gold price, convert the equivalent number of tokens to local currency, and pay the oil company. In that case Gold Bar Bank would accept the token back (as well as custody of equivalent amount of gold) and release money to the user's account in his preferred currency.

In a perfectly decentralized Blockchain-based application, the parties on the ledger would be as follows:

- Gold Bar Bank as the facilitator (all users would be registered here)

- Star Coffee Shop (or any other product or service provider organization)

Arab National Oil Company would be off-ledger, and hence it will not need membership or registration in this app.

Data

Data can fall into two different categories:

- **User/Organization data**: Data such as user ID, password, and node details will be stored on an off-chain database. Users are registered to the website post a stringent KYC process. Also, note that a user can be of two types: individual or organization. Individuals are any retail client, whereas an organization is any organization such as Star Coffee Shop that has an account on the platform and from where users can buy products.

- **Transactional data**: Details of user data, products data, trade data, and so on can only be shared between designated parties (e.g., Gold Bar Bank and Star Coffee Shop) where a transaction takes place.

For both these categories of data, all the details have to be elaborated by the business.

System architecture diagram

Below is a system diagram where approved users can register and login, after a stringent KYC process, to Gold Bar Bank and go ahead with the purchase of gold by converting them to utility tokens. Only user-specific data will be stored in the off-chain database, and all the transactional data will only be stored in the distributed ledger (Corda DLT here) platform for maximum security, privacy, and transparency between the authorized parties participating in the transactions.

Refer to *Figure 10.1* below. The Corda platform proposed here is a cutting-edge open-source Blockchain platform that removes costly friction in business transactions between organizations by enabling them to transact directly. Corda is the prime choice for insurance and banking domain for its unique distributed ledger architecture that has handled privacy of data most efficiently since its first release.

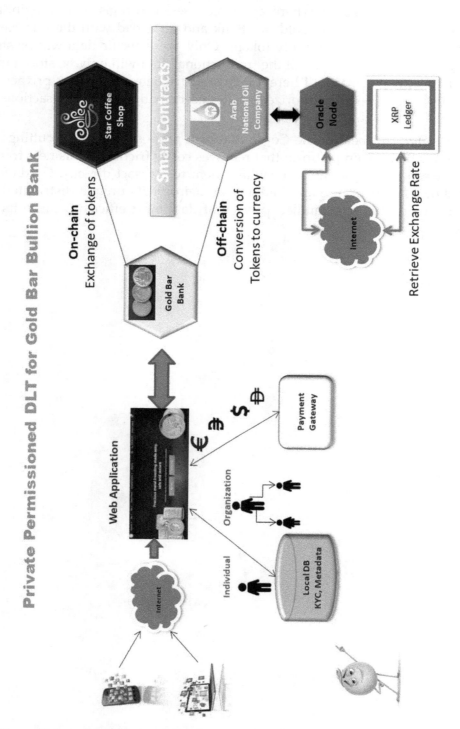

Figure 10.1: Architecture for applying Stablecoins/security tokens on distributed ledger

Transactions on Ledger

Interaction between off-chain and on-chain ledgers could occur in, but not limited to, the following cases:

1. **User account data management**: In this scenario, a new user's data is created and modified on the ledger by Gold Bar Bank. The new user is registered to Gold Bar Bank and purchases some gold. Now Gold Bar Bank creates an entry of the user to the ledger and populates it with user data such as user ID, name, and passport number, along with cash details in currency and the new tokens equivalent to the amount of gold the user has purchased from Gold Bar Bank. Ownership of data is with the user in association with Gold Bar Bank. The user, once registered, can push more money to his account or can buy more gold tokens. Hence, the number of tokens or cash balance can increase or decrease. In such a case, Gold Bar Bank would modify the data in the ledger against that user.

2. **Organization account data management**: Like a user, an organization such as Star Coffee Shop can also buy gold coins from Gold Bar Bank and sell them when no longer in need. In such cases, the ownership is with that organization.

3. **Account data deletion by user/organization**: In such a case, all the existing tokens would be transferred to Gold Bar Bank who would convert them to the user's currency and transfer to the user's/organization's account.

4. **Product data management by organization**: Products and services can be added to the ledger by an organization any time. This would include price in tokens and can be deleted when no longer needed.

5. **Purchase on-ledger**: Registered user on Gold Bar Bank purchases product or services from another organization (say Star Coffee Shop) that is on the ledger. In that case, a new trade takes place and both user and organization data are updated on the ledger with their respective tokens. Similarly, product data would be updated on the ledger, i.e., they would decrease in count with each purchase.

6. **Purchase off-ledger**: Registered user on Gold Bar Bank purchases product or services from another organization (say a petrol pump) that is not on the ledger. In that case, the current gold price is ascertained from the world market through a web service. The user's tokens are then converted to re-

quired currency by Gold Bar Bank who exchanges tokens for currency, and the currency is paid to the offline organization to purchase the product.

7. **Oracle web service call**: In a typical private-permissioned DLT, if there is a need for buying more gold tokens, a call invokes an external web service from the ledger to determine that day's gold price for conversion. For doing so, a neutral node known as oracle node is used, which works independently for all kinds of external calls or verification.

Smart contracts can be applied against each of these data modification in Corda DLT, as per the business requirement.

Advantages

As of now, use of crypto currencies such as Bitcoin is banned in quite a few countries, but stable utility coins could be the possible future; business houses can benefit by using tokenization for gold, renewable energy, or many such similar use cases. Let's discuss some of their benefits.

- Tokenization of collaterals gives peace of mind to investors and they may invest money early in the entire trading cycle. It is also a bright idea to engage users early in the business.

- Many rounds of authentication and authorization can be saved by automating and digitizing the dated processes in every step of the gold supply chain by using Blockchain as well as tokenization model of gold.

- Gold or oil or whatever commodity we use as a collateral is available at a much cheaper price owing to the elimination of middlemen.

- Trading of smaller quantities with no middleman can be introduced and enabled as divisibility could be very high with tokenization.

- Business transactions are transparent, where delivery against payment is achievable with a super-fast settlement speed in real time via the distributed ledger and tokenization of trusted collaterals.

Note: In case of collateral-backed tokenization, it is mandatory to organize regular auditing to check if the issuer (for example, Gold Bar Bank) actually has enough reserve as they claim.

Summary

In this chapter, we covered the following topics:

- Basics of Islamic finance

- Why most crypto currencies are banned or discouraged in Islamic world

- How Stablecoins can help

- Solution architecture for creating Stablecoins against valuables

- Advantages of Stablecoins

References

1. Islamic Finance market set to reach $3.25 trillion by 2020 - https://gulfnews.com/business/islamic-finance-market-set-to-reach-325-trillion-by-2020-1.1591447

2. Islamic Finance Basics – What is Murabaha, Ijara, and musharakah/mudarabah? - https://islamicfinanceaffairs.wordpress.com/2007/05/25/islamic-finance-basics-what-is-murabaha-ijara-and-musharakahmudarabah/

3. Blockchain and Crypto Asset Opportunities for Islamic Finance - https://coinsavage.com/content/2018/08/blockchain-crypto-asset-opportunities-for-islamic-finance/

4. Blockchain and Cryptoasset Opportunities for Islamic Finance - https://www.linkedin.com/pulse/blockchain-cryptoasset-opportunities-islamic-finance-matt-lunkes/

5. Validity of crypto currencies in Islamic finance? - https://www.dawn.com/news/1445072

Chapter 11

Banks of Tomorrow

So far we have discussed the history of payments and Ripple's architecture, its features, and development details with ample examples. We have also discussed Stablecoins and where they have been used so far. Now it's time to discuss how Ripple has been accepted in the market so far and who are the leaders and followers in this area. In this chapter, we will give readers insight into some of the biggest banks of the world, their strategies on adoption of Ripple, as well as a summary of countries moving towards Bank 4.0 by exploiting today's cutting-edge payment solutions. This chapter will be especially helpful for entrepreneurs and decision makers who always play safe and are still in *wait and watch* mode. They will be surprised to know how big a market Ripple has invaded so far and may be persuaded to invest in their strategy in this space.

Biggest banks of the world

Now let's see how some of the big names in the banking world are exploiting the benefits of Ripple and Stablecoins. **Forex Sentiment Board (FXSSI)** has categorized the banks of the world as per their total assets and market capitalization. *Listing 11.1* below shows the top 20 banks as of January 2019. [1]

Rank	Bank	Country	Asset
#1	**Industrial and Commercial Bank of China (ICBC)**	China	$4,009 billion
#2	China Construction Bank Corporation	China	$3,400 billion
#3	Agricultural Bank of China	China	$3,235 billion
#4	Bank of China ltd	China	$2,991 billion
#5	Mitsubishi UFJ Financial Group	Japan	$2,780 billion
#6	JPMorgan Chase	USA	$2,533 billion
#7	HSBC Holdings plc	England	$2,520 billion
#8	BNP Paribas	France	$2,357 billion
#9	Bank of America	USA	$2,281 billion
#10	Crédit Agricole	France	$2,117 billion
#11	Wells Fargo	USA	$1951 billion
#12	Japan Post Bank	Japan	$1874 billion
#13	Citigroup	USA	$1842 billion
#14	Sumitomo Mitsui Financial Group	Japan	$1775 billion
#15	Deutsche Bank	Germany	$1765 billion
#16	Banco Santander	Spain	$1736 billion
#17	Mizuho Financial Group	Japan	$1715 billion
#18	Barclays	England	$1532 billion
#19	Societe Generale	France	$1531 billion
#20	Groupe BPCE	France	$1512 billion

Listing 11.1: Biggest banks of the world

Also, it would be insightful to know who the top 100 banks in the world are and which country they belong to so that we can get a fair idea on their strategy for adoption of Ripple or Stablecoins. *Listing 11.2* shows a country-wise breakup of the details.

Rank	Country	Number of Banks in Top 100
-	European Union	36
1	China	18
2	United States	12
3	Japan	8
4	France	6
	United Kingdom	6
5	Canada	5
	Germany	5
	Spain	5
6	Australia	4
	Brazil	4
	South Korea	4
	Sweden	4
7	Italy	3
	Netherlands	3
	Singapore	3
8	Belgium	2
	Switzerland	2
9	Austria	1
	Denmark	1
	India	1
	Norway	1
	Russia	1
	Taiwan	1

Listing 11.2: Country-wise listing of banks in top 100

Live use cases: Continents and countries

When it comes to adoption of Ripple and Stablecoins for international remittance and currency exchange, it seems banks that used to be reluctant to use innovative technologies earlier are no more shying away. Let's find out who the leaders here are and who are the ones still waiting and watching to trade it safe sometime in future.

North America

USA ✓

JPMorgan Chase, the biggest bank in the USA, has already invested a fortune on JPM Coin that is largely appreciated by investors all over the world.

Citibank on the other hand has discarded any involvement in creating its own coin. However, they have not made it clear whether they would be using Ripple or SWIFT for futuristic remittance services.

American Express, another big bank from the USA, has taken a giant leap by integrating its payment services with Ripple's xCurrent to perform instant cross-border transactions and settlements. [2]

Wells Fargo is discussing the features of Ripple concerning payment processing technology and potential partnerships.

Headquartered in Dallas, USA, MoneyGram International Inc is the second largest provider of money transfers in the world, operating in more than two hundred countries with a giant global network of thousands of agent offices. In January 2018, MoneyGram announced partnership with Ripple to speed up fiat settlements. [3] Ripple has invested $50 million in MoneyGram as a take, and the latter is testing XRP and Ripple's xRapid for this purpose. [4]

The Western Union, an American worldwide financial services and communications company, might use Ripple (XRP) via Earthport, which is a Ripple client, although they might consider Cardano or Stellar Lumens as well. [5] As Western Union and VISA went into strategic partnership, VISA too might be using Ripple in future for currency transfer services.

Canada✓

In a report titled *Imagine 2025* published in September 2018, **Royal Bank of Canada (RBC)** has expressed its interest in evaluating Ripple products RippleNet, xCurrent, xRapid, and xVia to revolutionize the remittance and banking industries. [6] As per this report, RBC quotes,

"RippleNet can reduce the average banking costs by 46% per payment. On top of this, Ripple also provides transparency in terms of forex rates and fees, and easy tracking of funds which are features currently not available for cross-border inter-bank payments."

South America

Argentina and Brazil✓

As per a May 2019 report, Ripple has expanded its horizon to Latin America to their leading countries Argentina and Brazil with xRapid, a cross-border payment solution powered by XRP, ultimately promoting mass adoption of XRP. [7] More updates are awaited in this space.

Europe

England✓

As per recent news, HSBC (Banking Corporation of Hong Kong and Shanghai) has settled $250 billion in trades with a distributed ledger technology enabled by its Blockchain-based platform called HSBC FX Everywhere. [8]

The Standard Chartered Bank in England has already started pilot testing on RippleNet for moving real funds, with the objective of making cross-border payments. [9] [10]

Sweden✓

Skandinaviska Enskilda Banken AB (SEB), a Swedish financial group for corporate customers, has processed more than $1 billion in payments over RippleNet between Sweden and the USA. [11]

Germany✓

Deutsche Bank considers Ripple as a disruptor in the payment industry and has a close eye on Ripple developments. They are still relying on SWIFT gpi, considering its proven track record and stability in the market. [12]

France✓

French bank Crédit Agricole and many of its subsidiaries are testing Ripple's Blockchain to improve the efficiency of foreign exchange money transfers for regional banking customers who can use the services through their mobile devices. This process of international money transfer that used to take almost three days can be done almost instantly if the testing is successful. [13]

Spain✓

Spain-based Santander bank, which is also a leading bank of the world, is also using Ripple's xCurrent and RippleNet platform for remittance services. On March 23, 2019, Nathan Bostock, the UK CEO of Santander, said: "This spring, if not [sic] one beats us to it, we will be the first large retail bank to carry out cross-border payments at scale with Blockchain technology."

Oceania

Australia and New Zealand✓

In June 2018, the central banks of Australia and New Zealand commented that Bitcoin is insufficient and unsuitable for their operation. While they have expressed interest in adopting Ripple/XRP, Stellar Lumens, a close competitor, cannot be entirely ruled out. [14]

Asia

Japan✓

Tokyo-based SBI Holdings, also known as Strategic Business Innovator Group, is a leader in Ripple/XRP adoption among its contemporary FinTechs. In October 2018, SBI launched Blockchain-based payment application called MoneyTap using Ripple's xCurrent that would help domestic bank-to-bank transfers in *real time*. Users can use the Japanese yen or a few other fiat currencies of the world for the transfer without commission fees. Within Japan, almost thirteen banks have invested in SBI's Ripple-powered payment application. As per speculation, MoneyTap is expected to get participation from almost sixty-one Japanese banks in this product, representing more than 80% of the banks in the country. [15]

Japanese Bank Mitsubishi UFJ Financial group has already tested and showed its interest in Ripple/XRP system. [16] As per their statement, "In the current international remittance, we use a network of International Banking Communication Association (SWIFT) where financial institutions of each country participate. In many cases, it often goes through multiple banks; it takes a lot of fee and generally takes several days to remit . . . The successful launch of our commercial cross-border payment service marks a significant milestone in the financial industry's progress in applying distributed ledger technology for corporates." They have also mentioned, "We aim for practical use within a few years."

China ✓

As reported by the *South China Morning Post*, ICBC took over Wells Fargo to become the largest bank in the world by total assets as of January 2017. Although ICBC is investing largely in Blockchain technology, when it comes to finding cheaper, faster international money transfer solution, not much has been reported lately. The same is also true for China Construction Bank and Agricultural Bank of China, the other two major banks in China. Is crypto ban in China the reason? If so, they should reconsider their strategies and learn from other major players of the world. Innovations are simply impossible and growth is inhibited if such strict regulations are in practice. As an outcome, China, which is the banking leader of the world, might lose a huge opportunity in today's world.

While major banks in China are still in two minds about Ripple adoption, Lianlian Pay, a Chinese cross-border payment solution provider as well as the fourth largest non-banking third-party payment service provider in China, who has over 150 million registered customers, is helping American Express to process card payments in China and is considering XRP for doing so. [17]

Also, as per news on Forbes in January 2019, [18] "Ripple has finally managed to persuade a bank to adopt its XRP token. Euro Exim Bank, a London-based bank primarily focused on providing financial services for export and import companies . . . has signed up to use Ripple's xRapid service, for which XRP is the native token, for international customer payments." The reason behind Ripple adoption is the inefficiency of SWIFT network in solving modern-world demand of super-fast international remittances with a small amount of fee.

Thailand✓

Thailand's largest commercial bank Siam Commercial Bank (SCB) has undertaken several Blockchain-related initiatives to date. In September 2018, Ripple claimed, "Starting today, Siam Commercial Bank (SCB) will be the first financial institution on RippleNet to pioneer a key feature called 'multi-hop', which allows them to settle frictionless payments on behalf of other financial institutions on the network. This eliminates the need for a direct one-to-one connection (or bilateral relationship) between financial institutions to settle a payment. Using multi-hop, SCB will be able to receive and forward on a payment without a bilateral relationship between the originator and beneficiary institutions." However, as per recent news by FXStreet, [19] the Ripple integration is pretty much intact, although adoption of XRP has little clarity.

Kuwait✓

Kuwait Finance House Group, one of the leading Islamic banks in the Middle East, has recently announced the launch of Ripple-powered international remittances. As per the news, they would charge no fees for this service. [20] Surprise!

Saudi Arabia✓

The desert country South Arabia is a keen player in adopting latest technology for transfer of payments in global territory. Their Central Bank has partnered with Ripple to pilot instant cross-border payments on a blockchain, along with their domestic banks using Ripple's enterprise Blockchain solution xCurrent. [21]

UAE✓

As per a February 2018 report, UAE Exchange partnered with Ripple for international remittances. The exchange was reported as the largest payments firm in the Middle East to use RippleNet by the end of 2018 and announced that Blockchain-based remittances to Asia would be available by Q1 2019. [22]

India✓

Although there is huge confusion in crypto adoption in India, some players have already started working in this space and are well ahead of others.

Axis Bank in India introduced a Ripple-based international money transfer service back in 2017, which has reduced the time of transaction and settlement from three to five days to a few seconds. [23] As the news quotes,

"The bank has launched a service for its retail customers in India to receive payments from RAKBANK in UAE and for its corporate customers in India to receive payments from Standard Chartered Bank in Singapore."

It's worth noting that Axis is the third biggest bank in India in the private sector and has been a pioneer in adopting changes in international remittance.

Yes Bank, the fourth largest private sector bank in India, is not far behind. In an article published in September 2018, [24] the bank has announced its interest in Ripple/XRP for real-time cross-border payments.

In February 2018, Mumbai-based new-generation bank, IndusInd Bank, has expressed its interest in Ripple products for cross-border remittance. [25]

In 2018, Kotak Mahindra Bank as well has started experimenting with Ripple's xCurrent for instant money transfer into the country. [26]

As per a news article in March 2019, "India's Federal Bank Partners with Ripple to Accelerate Cross-Border Remittances." [27]

Crypto ban in India!

As the biggest receiver of remittance services, India can largely benefit from Ripple adoption. But is crypto currency not banned by the Reserve Bank of India (RBI)? Ok, let's rather say that at least for some time the Indian government is considering its strategies on accepting crypto currency. And the good news is that (as shown in *Figure 11.1* below), unlike other crypto currencies like Bitcoin, Ripple is unfazed by such regulation. [28]

Ripple sees life beyond RBI cryptocurrency ban

Mayur Shetty | TNN | Updated: Jun 21, 2018, 13:31 IST   ✉ 🖶   A-   A+

MUMBAI: Fintech company Ripple, which straddles the world of cryptocurrencies and cross-border remittances, is unfazed by the Reserve Bank of India's (RBI's) restriction on banks dealing with cryptocurrencies. The company is betting on Basel norms and the RBI's own panel report on digital currencies for a new framework that could lead to rescinding the ban.

"Ripple's global head of infrastructure innovation Dilip Rao said that unlike Bitcoin and cryptocurrencies, Ripple plans to use the Interledger protocol – the payments protocol created by Ripple, to enable remittance of fiat currency and not to replace it." Besides using XRP for remittance, The company also offers its platform Ripple Network to lenders for facilitating cross-border remittances — rivalling the SWIFT network that has been conventionally used by banks.

Ripple has tied up with private lenders Yes Bank, Axis Bank and IndusInd for using the blockchain-based platform for payments without the use of the cryptocurrency asset. It, however, maintains that it aims to use XRP in future as a 'connecting cryptocurrency' to facilitate remittance.

Last year, Ripple had also set up an office in Mumbai and appointed former Citibanker Navin Gupta as country manager. "There is a great regulatory comfort with Ripple Net — particularly in the light of the Bank for International Settlements' policy requiring central banks to have a backup for payment systems having non-similar technology," said Rao. He added that this was crucial as payment systems were systemically important and a cyber-attack to systems would be akin to infection of the core. In India, while the RBI has barred banks from servicing companies dealing in cryptocurrencies, it has also set up a panel to look into the possibility of a central bank digital currency.

"Even from a geopolitical point of view, countries are having concerns over the existing cross-border payment systems, which can be switched off with a turn of the switch," said Rao. In addition to pitching Ripple for cross-border payments, the company is offering its own platform as an alternative to Real Time Gross Settlement (RTGS) system for countries that do not have a developed interbank network.

Figure 11.1: Ripple ban in India!

As per a news report in June 2018, Ripple will facilitate remittance in existing fiat currencies and does not intend to replace them. Hope readers from neighboring countries who have banned all crypto currencies are listening!

Conclusion

As a panelist at a global conference on emerging technologies held in the USA, I discussed some of the latest developments in this space and also quoted some projects I am involved in that use R3 Corda distributed ledger and Ripple. It surprised me when some of the business leaders approached me afterwards for a quick chat and conveyed their skepticism; in fact, most of them were in two minds on Ripple adoption. "Ripple is too risky, and post Bitcoin meltdown, only a handful are experimenting with this volatile crypto" was the general public view. That incident inspired me to write this book, and especially this entire chapter that focuses on Ripple's status in the market as of July 2019.

As shown in *Figure 11.2*, Ripple has not only secured a strong position in most countries and continents of the world, but has also scored its position on Forbes' top 50 start-ups both in 2018 [29] and 2019 [30] as a Blockchain and FinTech company.

BLOCKCHAIN

- 50 -

Allianz SE	Facebook	Nestle
Amazon	Fidelity	Northern Trust
Anheuser-Busch Inbev	Foxconn	Oracle
Ant Financial	Golden State Foods	Overstock
BBVA	Google	PNC
Bitfury	HPE	Ripple
BNP Paribas	HTC	Samsung
BP PLC	IBM	Santander
Broadridge	ING	SAP SE
Bumble Bee Foods	Intel	Seagate Technology
Cargill	JPMorgan Chase	Siemens
Ciox Health	Maersk	Signature Bank
Citigroup	Mastercard	State Farm
Coinbase	Metlife	UBS
Comcast	Microsoft	Visa
CVS Health	Nasdaq	VMware
DTCC		Walmart

Figure 11.2: Top 50 Blockchain companies in world by Forbes. Pic Source: [31]

In fact, slowly and steadily, continent by continent, country by country, bank by bank, and FinTech by FinTech, Ripple is moving towards mass adoption.

As per a news report on May 17, 2019, "World's Largest Banks [are] Investing $50M in Digital Cash Settlement System", [32] many of which we have already discussed in this book.

As per a Finextra report back in 2016, people across the world send more than $155 trillion across borders, and this number is on an exponential rise year after year. [33] As per a report in April 2019 by Business Standard, World Bank quoted that India retains the top spot with largest remittances globally: [34]

"India retained its top spot on remittances with 79 billion dollars followed by China (67 billion dollars), Mexico (36 billion dollars), the Philippines (34 billion dollars) and Egypt (29 billion dollars)."

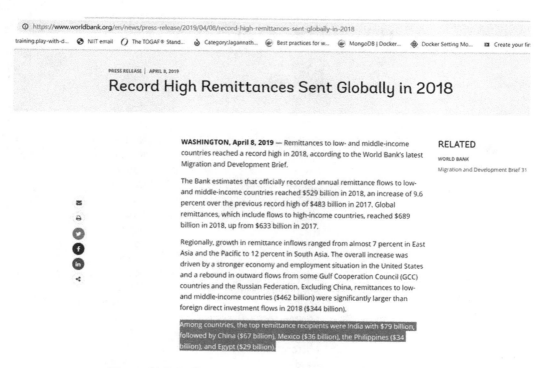

Figure 11.3: India No. 1 receiver of international remittance

Remittance is a huge issue for India and other countries in this list who still use age-old, flawed remittance systems with a settlement time of few days, and it's high time that these banks and financial institutions re-evaluate their existing payment mechanism to stay relevant in the current market.

Among so many developments as well as speculations, one question that regularly arises is, what will be the future of banking? Well, even if it's too much of a challenge to predict the exact functioning of banking and payment industry in the next century, at least for the next decade, we are definitely going to experience a mammoth transformation. Banks and FinTechs must be much more flexible in adopting these latest practices for building a frictionless, real-time global payment system, and many have already started working on it.

Summary

In this chapter, we covered the following topics:

- Biggest banks of the world and the countries they reside in

- Ripple adopters in continents and countries across the world

- Ripple adoption in India even after crypto ban

- Why India should invest more on Ripple

- Mass adoption of Ripple in future

References

1. TOP 20 Largest World Banks in 2019 by Total Assets - https://fxssi.com/top-20-largest-world-banks-in-current-year

2. American Express deepens ties with Ripple, confirms using its xCurrent Blockchain Solution - https://www.coinspeaker.com/american-express-deepens-ties-ripple-confirms-using-xcurrent-blockchain-solution/

3. Ripple announces partnership with MoneyGram to speed Fiat Settlements - https://cointelegraph.com/news/ripple-announces-partnership-with-moneygram-to-speed-fiat-settlements

4. Ripple and MoneyGram Test XRP Currency Transfers - https://cryptocoinmastery.com/ripple-moneygram-test-xrp-currency-transfers/

5. Western Union might use Ripple (XRP) via Earthport now - https://www.tronweekly.com/western-union-might-use-ripple-via-earthport/

6. Royal Bank Of Canada Endorses Ripple as Future of the Remittance Industry - https://www.bitrates.com/news/p/royal-bank-of-canada-endorses-ripple-as-future-of-the-remittance-industry

7. Ripple Pushes Its XRP-Powered xRapid Solution to Argentina and Brazil - https://www.coinspeaker.com/ripple-xrapid-argentina-brazil/

8. Using Ripple & DLT, HSBC Settles $250b Foreign Exchange Transactions, Proves RippleNet Efficiency - https://todaysgazette.com/using-ripple-dlt-hsbc-settles-250b-foreign-exchange-transactions-proves-ripplenet-efficiency/

9. Cross-Border Payment Pilot Test - https://www.sc.com/en/media/press-release/cross-border-payment-pilot-test/

10. Standard Chartered to extend use of RippleNet to more countries - https://www.finextra.com/newsarticle/32048/standard-chartered-to-extend-use-of-ripplenet-to-more-countries

11. RippleNet Grows To 100 Financial Institutions - https://www.pymnts.com/blockchain/2017/ripplenet-blockchain-network-grows-to-100-financial-institutions/

12. Deutsche Bank on Ripple and SWIFT gpi - https://www.paymenteye.com/2018/06/15/deutsche-bank-on-ripple-and-swift-gpi/

13. This French bank is testing international money transfers on Ripple's Blockchain - https://www.finder.com/this-french-bank-is-testing-international-money-transfers-on-ripples-blockchain

14. Central Banks of New Zealand and Australia to Adopt Ripple Soon? - https://ripplenews.tech/2018/06/28/central-banks-new-zealand-australia-adopt-ripple-soon/

15. Siam Commercial Bank Pioneers RippleNet's *Multi-hop* Feature - https://ripple.com/insights/siam-commercial-bank-pioneers-ripplenets-multi-hop-feature/

16. Ripple (XRP) and Mitsubishi: Ripple's Solutions Tested and Loved by Many - https://ethereumworldnews.com/ripple-xrp-and-mitsubishi-ripples-solutions-tested-and-loved-by-many/

17. Ripple's XRP could soon be used to make payments in China - https://cyclicmint.com/ripples-xrp-could-soon-be-used-to-make-payments-in-china/

18. Ripple Has Signed Up A Bank To Use XRP For Payments. So What? - https://www.forbes.com/sites/francescoppola/2019/01/29/ripple-has-signed-up-a-bank-to-use-xrp-for-payments-so-what/#42dda0c61084

19. Thailand's Siam Commercial Bank to use Ripple Blockchain; XRP to wait for the announcement - https://www.fxstreet.com/cryptocurrencies/news/thailands-siam-commercial-bank-to-use-ripple-blockchain-xrp-to-wait-for-the-announcement-201905231001

20. Ripple to power "Instant International Transfer" for Kuwait's KFH bank - https://www.fxstreet.com/cryptocurrencies/news/ripple-to-power-instant-international-transfer-for-kuwaits-kfh-bank-201901070800

21. Ripple Partners Saudi Arabia's Central Bank to Plug Banks on a Blockchain - https://www.ccn.com/ripple-partners-saudi-arabias-central-bank-plug-banks-blockchain/

22. UAE Exchange and Payment Platform Unimoni Join Ripple's Payments Network - https://cointelegraph.com/news/uae-exchange-and-payment-platform-unimoni-join-ripples-payments-network

23. Axis Bank launches ripple-powered instant payment service for retail and corporate customers -https://www.thehindubusinessline.com/business-wire/axis-bank-launches-ripplepowered-instant-payment-service-for-retail-and-corporate-customers/article9973516.ece

24. Impact on Real-Time Cross-Border Payments - https://www.yesbank.in/digital-banking/tech-for-change/financial-services/impact-on-realtime-cross-border-payments

25. IndusInd Bank and Ripple tie up for Cross Border Remittances - https://www.indusind.com/iblogs/pressrelease/indusind-bank-ripple-tie-cross-border-remittances

26. India's Kotak Mahindra Bank taps Ripple xCurrent for remittances - https://www.finextra.com/newsarticle/32320/indias-kotak-mahindra-bank-taps-ripple-xcurrent-for-remittances

27. Federal Bank Ltd. - Federal Bank Partners Ripple To Accelerate Cross-Border Remittances - Intimation Under Regulation 30 Pursuant To SEBI (Listing Obligations And Disclosure Requirements) Regulations, 2015 - https://www.thehindubusinessline.com/companies/announcements/others/federal-bank-ltd-federal-bank-partners-ripple-to-accelerate-cross-border-remittances-intimation-under-regulation-30-pursuant-to-sebi-listing-obligations-and-disclosure-requirements-regulations-2015/article26666101.ece

28. Ripple sees life beyond RBI crypto currency ban - https://timesofindia.indiatimes.com/business/india-business/ripple-sees-life-beyond-rbi-cryptocurrency-ban/articleshow/64594035.cms

29. Coinbase, Gemini, and Ripple Named Among LinkedIn's Top 50 Startups of 2018 - https://bitcoinexchangeguide.com/coinbase-gemini-and-ripple-named-among-linkedins-top-50-startups-of-2018/

30. Forbes 'Fintech 50 Rundown' Features Coinbase, Gemini, Ripple, Circle, Bitfury and Axoni Crypto Companies - https://bitcoinexchangeguide.com/forbes-fintech-50-rundown-features-coinbase-gemini-ripple-circle-bitfury-and-axoni-crypto-companies/

31. Blockchain 50: Billion Dollar Babies - https://www.forbes.com/sites/michaeldelcastillo/2019/04/16/blockchain-50-billion-dollar-babies/#677c632957cc

32. World's Largest Banks Investing $50M in Digital Cash Settlement System - https://www.coinspeaker.com/banks-50-m-digital-cash-settlement/

33. Ripple scores $55 million funding round; adds new bank members - https://www.finextra.com/newsarticle/29445/ripple-scores-55-million-funding-round-adds-new-bank-members

34. Record High Remittances Sent Globally in 2018 - https://www.worldbank.org/en/news/press-release/2019/04/08/record-high-remittances-sent-globally-in-2018

Some other great resources for reference are as follows:

1. SBI Reports Financial Results, Recognizes Ripple for Cross Border Payments - https://cointelegraph.com/news/sbi-reports-financial-results-recognizes-ripple-for-cross-border-payments

2. Panel *Let's send the money!* at Paris FinTech Forum 2019 with Brad Garlinghouse, CEO, Ripple, (United States) and Gottfried Leibbrandt, CEO, SWIFT, (Belgium) - https://www.youtube.com/watch?v=SRoCGr4cess

Index

A

account information (account_info)
  retrieving 56-58
Amazon
  about 89
  URL 89

B

banking world 149, 151
Bank of Singapore (DBS) 124
banks
  credibility, after crisis 4
  evolution 3, 4
Binance GBP 134
Bitcoin
  about 6
  criteria, for cross-border
      remittance 6, 7
Blockchain
  advantages 8-10

Blockchain solution 104, 106, 123
Blockchain technology
  about 7
  features 7
business insured
  obtaining 117
business process flow 118-120
business scenario 93, 104

C

capital market 102
charity 91
CheckCash 122
checks 79, 80
ChequeCancel transaction type 122
coin5s
  URL 13
Corda Settler 96
cross-currency payments
  about 71, 72

reference link 72
crypto currencies
  in Islamic finance 140
  Islamic version 140
crypto currency
  banned, in india 157, 158
crypto currency (XRP) 12-14, 33
currency codes
  reference link 34

D

data
  about 142
  transactional data 142
  user/organization data 142
decentralized exchange 71
derivatives
  challenges 111, 112
  scenario 113
  solution 112
derivatives, types
  about 109
  forward 110
  futures 110
  options 110
  swaps 111
  warrants 111
Digix Gold (DGX) 129
distributed ledger 45, 46
drop 34

E

e-Auction
  challenges 94

e-Auction, use case
  fraud 95
  limited participation 95
  long settlement 95
Energy Block Exchange (EBX) 98
EscrowCreate transaction type 122
Escrow payment
  about 72
  process 73-78
European Central Bank (ECB) 103

F

FinTechs
  on XRP ecosystem 19
forex rate
  about 97
  reference link 97
Forex Sentiment Board (FXSSI) 149

G

General Data Protection
    Regulation (GDPR) 46
Gold Bar Bank 141
Gold tokenization
  about 141
  advantages 146

H

hardware wallet 83

I

illegal use case 70
initial product offering (IPO) 94

instant settlement
  about 95
  advantages 98
interbank money transfer 24, 25
Interledger Protocol (ILP) 37
internal capital adequacy assessment
    process (ICAAP) 103
internal liquidity adequacy assess-
    ment process (ILAAP) 103
international money transfer 25
international remittance
  about 23
  working 23
international trading
  challenges 120
  currency 121
  parties 121
  payment 121
  solution 121
intrabank money transfer 24
IoT messaging 90
Islamic banking 139, 140
issued currencies
  about 34
  freezing 35

J

JSON request
  reference link 57

L

Ledger
  transactions 145, 146
legal use case 71
letter of credit (LoC) 118

letter of intent (LoI) 132
limit order 93
Live Use case
  continents and countries 156
Live Use Case
  about 124
  continents and countries 152-157
  Euro Exim Bank 124
  Standard Charted Bank 124
local rippled server
  executing 56
local rippled validating server
  executing 55

M

manufacturing and payment risks
  mitigating 117
market order 94
microfinance 91
micropayments
  challenges 90
  examples 90
mobile wallet 83
modern banking system
  pain points 4
money market
  about 102
  challenges 103
  for intraday trading 103

N

nostro accounts
  about 27
  liquidity issue 30, 31

P

partial payment 69, 70

pay-as-you-go services 91

payment channels 81, 82

Payment object 69

payments
  history 1, 2

PayPal 89

Petroleum trade
  use case 115-117

Pre-Blockchain money
      transfer solutions 5

Proof of Work (PoW) 32

R

R3 Corda
  about 44
  features 46-49

real-time gross
      settlement (RTGS) 104, 131

request for quote (RFQ) 104

Ripple
  about 10, 11, 15, 31, 44
  advantages 14, 15, 107, 113
  cons 135
  disadvantages 15
  key benefits 98, 99
  misconceptions 15-18
  pros 135
  unknown facts 15-18
  using 42
  versus Stablecoins 135
  versus SWIFT 43

Ripple Consensus Ledger (RCL) 11

rippled server 33

rippled server, types
  server, validating 33
  stand-alone mode 33
  stock server 33
  validator 33

Ripple, financial markets
  capital market 43
  equity market 43
  forex market 43
  money market 43

ripple library
  download link 61

RippleNet 35

Ripple protocol consensus
      algorithm (RPCA) 32

Ripple solution
  about 95
  Ripple-based settlement 96
  Tokenization model 96

Ripple's XRP Ledger
  advantages 122

Ripple/XRP
  solution 91

S

smart contracts 146

Society for Worldwide Interbank
      Financial Telecommunication
      (SWIFT) 23

software wallet 83

Stablecoins
  about 127-131
  by Binance 134
  by Facebook 132, 133

by JPMorgan 131, 132
by Swiss Stock Exchange 134
cons 135, 136
pros 135
Tether 131
versus Ripple 135
Stablecoins, types
about 128
backed by crypto currency 130
backed by fiat currency 129
backed by no collateral 130
backed by valuable collaterals 129
stop order 94
SWIFT
about 26-28
versus Ripple 43
SWIFT codes 26
SWIFT currency codes 26
SWIFT global payment
innovation (gpi) 29
SWIFT pain points 28, 29
SwissRealCoin (SRC) 129
Swiss Stock Exchange (SIX) 134
system architecture diagram 143

T

Testnet faucet
reference link 53
Testnet network
reference link 53
Tether 131
tfPartialPayment 69
Toast Wallet 83
tokenization model 96
trade finance 115

transactions per second (TPS) 11

U

unique node list (UNL) 32

V

vostro accounts 27

W

Websocket request 78
World Wide Web
Consortium (W3C) 39

X

xCurrent 4.0 41, 42
xCurrent (full access) 37, 39
xCurrent (full access),
building blocks
FX Ticker 39
ILP Ledger 39
messenger 38
validator 38
xRapid 40, 41
XRP
for micropayments 92
XRP account
account information (account_info),
retrieving 56-58
creating, in production 83
creating, in Testnet 53, 54
factors 54, 55
local rippled validating server,
executing 55, 56
XRP Ledger endpoints 56
XRP Ledger endpoints 56

XRP Ledger, payment structure
  reference link 63
XRP Ledger test network, checks
  reference link 81
XRP Ledger (XRPL)
  about 11, 31
  consensus in 31, 32
  reference link 56
XRPs
  buying 84, 85
  sending 84
  transferring, between
    accounts 60-68
xVia (standard access) 36

CPSIA information can be obtained
at www.ICGtesting.com
Printed in the USA
FFHW011332131219
56976586-62598FF